Privilege of the Platform

Books Available by Dan Clark:

Forgotten Fundamentals—The Answers Are in the Box
Best or Right—Why Great Is Not Good Enough
The Art of Execution
Chicken Soup for the College Soul
Puppies for Sale and Other Inspirational Tales
Puppies for Sale (Illustrated Storybook)
Clark's Children's Classics
Soul Food, Volumes I and II (Dan's Complete Story Collection)
The Funniest Things Happen When You Look for Laughs
The Thrill of Teaching
The Book of Wisdom, Rhymes, and Wizardry
Rainbows Follow Rain
Lyrical Poetry
Only the Best on Leadership
Only the Best on Customer Service

Order at his web site: www.danclarkspeak.com

Privilege of the Platform

The Art and Science of Public Speaking

By the National Speakers Association
Hall-of-Fame Speaker

Dan Clark, CSP, CPAE

CFI
Springville, Utah

ISBN 13: 978-1-59955-054-1

Published by CFI, an imprint of Cedar Fort, Inc., 2373 W. 700 S., Springville, UT, 84663
Distributed by Cedar Fort, Inc. www.cedarfort.com

Cover design by Nicole Williams
Cover design © 2007 by Lyle Mortimer
Edited and typeset by Annaliese B. Cox

Photgraphs by Scott Campbell

Printed in the United States of America

10 9 8 7 6 5 4 3 2 1

Printed on acid-free paper

Our chief want is someone who will inspire us to be what we know we could become.

—Ralph Waldo Emerson

Put it before them briefly so they will read it, clearly so they will appreciate it, picturesquely so they will remember it, and accurately so they will be guided by its light.

—Joseph Pulitzer

The goal in every presentation is to have people leave impressed with themselves, impressed with what they now know that they didn't know before, impressed with what they now can do that they could not do before.

—Bob Pike,
Professional Speaker

Table of Contents

ACKNOWLEDGMENTS

For my special teachers who believed in me when others wouldn't: Ms. Dubois, Mrs. Inman, Dr. Morray, Mrs. Smart, Principal Richards, Mr. Croft, Mr. Thorem and Coaches Din Morris, Brooks, Allen, Wageman, Trost, Martin, Weight, Simons, Banker, Zimmer, McBride, and Gadd.

For Russ Anderson, Don Pugh, Doug Miller, Fran Peak, Dick Nourse, Zig Ziglar, Jim and Karen Koeninger, Norm Gibbons, Lila Bjorkland, Micky Fisher, Jennifer Lapine, Ernie Wilhoit, Don Wilson, Kay Baker, Pat Mutch, Steve Cosgrove, Les Hewitt, Don Gale, Michael Gale, Chuck Coonradt, Charles Reid, Steve Munn, Wayne and Ruby Clark, Paul Clark, Kelly Clark, Gen. Hal Hornburg (Ret.), Maj. Gen. Johnny Weida, and Laura Calchera (Supreme Commander) for helping me launch my career and/or take it to the next level.

For my National Speakers Association inspiration: Mark Victor Hansen, Jack Canfield, Gail Larsen, Naomi Rhode, Dave Gordon, Robert Henry, Renee Strom, Keith Harrell, Roger Crawford, Bubba Bechtol, Grady Jim Robinson, Jim Tunney, Jeanne Robertson, Bob Murphy, Patricia Fripp, Ray Pelletier, Max Dixon, Mark Sanborn, and Art Berg.

For Bill Kimball, Bob and Paul Mendenhall, Dick Clissold, Bill Gibbs, Jay Jensen, Bob Raybould, Lincoln Hanks, Pres. Royden and Sister Derrick, Phillip Gibson, Mark Tuttle, Gary Mangum, Scott Buie, Mark Monsen, Mont Beardall, Blain Hope, Todd Petersen, Colin and Theresa Dunne, Brendan and Evelyn Gibney, Todd Morgan, Brad Morris, and Brent Bowen for your spirituality, commitment to obedience, faith, and influence in my Christian walk with God.

For K.C., Danny, Nikola, McCall, and Alexandrea for finding wisdom, comfort, laughter, and solace in my speeches, stories, anecdotes, and words. I love you and need you in my life forever.

Preface

Everybody knows that one person can change the course of history—George Washington, Abraham Lincoln, Mahatma Gandhi, Winston Churchill, and Martin Luther King Jr. are all examples of that. From the likes of Tiger Woods and what he did with golf, we know that one person can transform an entire industry. This holds true in the world of professional speaking. The title of this book, *Privilege of the Platform*, is a phrase that was coined and created by a former president of the National Speakers Association, the sophisticated, elegant, polished, and professional Naomi Rhode. Naomi is one of those charismatic individuals spoken of who has influenced her industry forever as a role model for every speaker who knows her.

As mentioned, in her year as president of NSA, Naomi chose for her tenured theme "The Privilege of the Platform." It epitomizes the significant responsibility each one of us has whenever we are given the opportunity to speak in public. It had a powerful effect on me then and still does to this day as it serves as a constant reminder to never take for granted any opportunity to touch someone's life. Because she has influenced so many, I am inspired to also do my part in whatever way I can.

Since 1982, I have been a full-time professional speaker. In contrast with my three siblings—who own a large insurance agency, successfully sell real estate, and manage a prestigious investment banking firm—when my mother is asked what I do, she answers, "Dan? Oh, he talks. We're so proud." Speaking for a living is a curious profession, and one that has been very good to me. Not only has it taken me all over the world and allowed me to share the platform with some of the most powerful, interesting, and famous people on our planet, but it has also given me the opportunity to positively touch people's lives and change the world one story at a time. My mom proudly brags that I am "the best speech she ever delivered!"

In the attitude of "giving back," and because so many people are like the tiny child standing on his tiptoes, craning his neck to peer up on the table to see what all the colorful things are, I have penned this comprehensive guide on the art and science of speaking in public. The following chapters include twelve of the most frequently asked questions about public speaking, along with my answers, and will allow me to teach everything I know about presentations, preparation, interviewing, crafting a speech, facilitating small group interactive training, and keynoting to a huge group on a big stage with large-room platform skills. So that you won't have to pass through the same tight spaces that I did to become a good communicator, and because I am buoyed up by the thought that in my twenty-five plus years as a professional speaker I have actually acquired some knowledge and experience that is worth sharing on this subject, and because there might be someone—you—out there who will enter into this magnificent profession as a result of my sharing, I present this book.

Must-Read Introduction

When I was in college, one professor required that we read *Oedipus Rex* by Sophocles. The most memorable yet twisted part of the play for me is when Oedipus unknowingly does some terrible things, and when he realizes it, he feels that the only way he can make amends is to be punished. Consequently, he blinds himself. The thought that someone would deliberately blind himself not only troubled me when I read it, but it has remained a source of internal excavation ever since, especially now that I am a professional speaker. Having a job that encompasses teaching, inspiring, influencing, guiding, and taking people's hearts to places their minds can never go has not only made me more aware of how many misguided, shortsighted, and blatantly "blind" people there are among us, but it has reintroduced me to a familiar quote, rekindled a curiosity to deepen my understanding of it and recommit to never letting it happen to me. "When the blind lead the blind, they both fall into the ditch," obviously refers to mental, emotional, topical, moral, ethical, and spiritual blindness. At first glance, the focus of this truism seems to be about the perils that come to a follower who has been blinded by the craftiness of a blind, charismatic leader. In a larger corporate, association, church, or school sense, behavioral anthropologists call this blindness "social proof," where we are emotionally moved to follow the crowd because there is strength in numbers and everybody else is following the ever-growing crowd.

In the context of this book, I want to focus on the other side of the "blind leading the blind" involving those in the lead whose mission it is to help their blind followers and listeners to see. Obviously when a manager, educator, preacher, or speaker is blind they cannot fulfill this responsibility, and it's only a matter of time before they find themselves and their people in the "ditches" of life. Of course, some claim their blindness is because they had a blind leader perpetuate what their blind leader perpetuated and they don't know any better than to also pass this blindness along. But we all know this is the exception, not the rule. Most blind leaders suffer from the same self-inflicted blindness evidenced in our own lives when we refuse to see the danger or evil in our choice of beliefs, friends, business interests, influences, health habits, and environments. Each of us could avoid the pain that inevitably results from such self-deception if we would simply let go of traditions based on who is right, and start developing convictions based on what is right. Bad eyesight can always be corrected with good insight.

I often see this self-inflicted "Oedipus blindness" in the world of professional speaking. The unwritten expectation of the National Speakers Association is that all members will become "polished," and as one who respects and fully supports NSA, I have relentlessly pursued this classification for nearly three decades. Where the blindness occurs is in the misinterpretation of what "polished" means. I have seen too many so-called polished speakers bomb in their speeches. Why? How can this happen? Simply, some of the biggest wigs in professional speaking have turned a blind eye to the true definition of "polished" and have perpetuated it. If polished means a completely memorized speech with choreographed movements, practiced punctuated pauses, forced gestures, imitated voice inflections, and no desire for spontaneity, then being polished only makes you an accomplished actor starring in your own play. Sure they loved you in Chicago on Thursday, but you didn't connect with your Orlando audience on Saturday. Is it their fault? No! You have been blinded by a motivation to make a speech rather than to make a difference. These are the speakers referred to as "slick" who give the profession a bad name; the "soothsayers" who say soothing things the same smooth way every single time. These are not the extraordinary speakers. They are merely polished presenters.

However, if "polished" means you have taken the time to think through what you believe, why you believe it, and what you know that will help others succeed, you realize that your words of wisdom are not a hypocritical hoax, but rather a natural exposure of your passion for living that is the real you offstage. And as you talk with one person at a time—regardless of the size of the audience—and as you make direct eye contact; use natural gestures; allow conversational pauses to let the audience laugh, think, feel, and cry; and are spontaneous because you are carrying on a vulnerable inspirational conversation with your audience members as if you are out to dinner rather than on a stage, then you are an accomplished, consummate communicator who will never bomb. You are one of the extraordinary individuals who can take pride in calling yourself a polished speaker. When you have reached this level, with the right coach you now can continue to polish and become more of who you already are by injecting colorful metaphors, simile, irony, alliteration, descriptive action verbs, and more humor and emotion into your speaking. When this is achieved, you have earned the title of "polished professional speaker" and are ready to speak for a living. In this context, polished refers not to the end of a speech, but rather to the continual transformational "polishing" that occurs during your speech where you move from *hyper* entertainer, to *helper* with their needs, to *healer* of their pain, to *host* of their new possibilities.

Although I discuss this in greater detail in the book, I wanted to "begin with this end in mind" to make sure that every page you read carries with it the underlying message that we must "be" before we "do"; that when we identify ourselves in terms of what we do instead of who we are, we become human doings instead of human beings—unacceptable if authentic, honest communication and deeper, meaningful connection is what we seek. "Slick" polished presenters are self-centered and egocentric, obviously focusing on themselves and their performance skills to do and say things right. True polished speakers, however, are service-centered and customer-centric, focusing on the audience, on being themselves, being present in the moment, and saying the right things. Of course there is an art to public speaking and a science to preparing a speech, but both success and failure boil down to only one question: What kind of communicator do you want to be? Will you open your eyes and free your personality to be the speaker you have the capacity to be? Or like Oedipus, will you self-inflict a blindness that holds you hostage to the mechanical role of doing what mere presenters do? By the end of this book you will SEE what I mean!

Chapter 1

Is Communication an Art?

Dr. Bill Magee, world renowned plastic surgeon and founder of the international humanitarian medical organization called Operation Smile, teaches that reason leads to conclusions, but that it is emotion that leads to action. Reason is logical, headstrong, and the metaphorical, surgical procedure required to repair the wounded parts of our lives. Emotion is felt, heart-strong, and the healing process required to fully benefit from the corrective procedure. Reason implies a scientific approach; emotion implies an artful approach. Both are equally important; both are needed. One without the other is like a kiss without a squeeze, a dance song without a dancer, a photo op without a camera.

In a book subtitled "The Art and Science of Public Speaking," one would assume that all of this and more would be covered; that is, if the definition of each title word is accurate, clear, agreed upon, and recalled when reading. My understanding is: The need to speak in public implies that a group of people have gathered in a meeting where at least one of them is qualified to address the group and consequently is asked to do so with an expected power and eloquence. Because it is not what we do but who we do it with that makes or breaks us, and no one can take themselves to the next level all by themselves, it is critical to be willing to pay any price and travel any distance to associate with extraordinary human beings. Hence, the need for supportive, informative, and inspiring meetings. There is strength in numbers, and therefore, we should come together in a common purpose as often as possible to rededicate ourselves to a formulated plan. This is where art and science come into play and the necessity for both to constantly and interdependently interface becomes obvious.

An artful approach to anything in life is about focusing on purposes instead of just setting goals. A scientific approach only stresses goals. Science is evidence-based and fueled by facts, formulas, and obedience to the letter-of-the-law with a belief that things happen for a reason. Art is emotion-based and fueled by passion, imagination, and sensitivity to the spirit-of-the-law with a conviction that, yes, things happen for a reason, but it is our responsibility to determine what that reason is. Science states "self" is discovered; art states that "self" is created. A scientific approach comes from the left-brain, cognitive, logical side of our minds with a desire for a specific step-by-step strategy. An artful approach comes from the right-brain, relational, feeling side of our minds with a desire for spontaneity. An artful approach focuses on answering "why should I do it?" while a scientific approach focuses on "how to do it." Ironically, as we amalgamate them into the same desired result, when we identify our why's, figuring out the how-to's becomes a simple and exhilarating task. Bottom line: In the absence of purpose there is no plan; in the absence of reason there is no direction; in the absence of emotion there is no change; and with no desire or need to change, there is no reason to seek out extraordinary individuals who will inspire us to live on purpose. And this self-perpetuating cycle of personal and professional development begins all over again.

With this understanding of the importance of holding meetings with engaging speakers who understand the difference between art and science, let us shift our emphasis from talking to communicating and, specifically, to the question at hand: "Is communication an art?"

Communication is more than just two or more people taking turns talking. And it's definitely not thinking about what you are going to say next while waiting for the person who is currently talking to take a breath so that you can jump in with another of your "two cents." As Steven Covey teaches in *The 7 Habits of Highly Effective People*, "Seek first to understand, then to be understood." Communication is simply the clear understanding in a common language between two or more individuals.

A young mother was in her home talking on the phone. Somehow, her little four-year-old boy had managed to open the front door and wander out onto the sidewalk. As the mom looked out the window, she saw her son standing at the edge of their busy street with cars, trucks, and buses whipping by. Frantically, she dropped the phone, sprinted to the intersection, and picked him up just before he stepped out into oncoming traffic.

First hugging him and then holding him at arm's length, she scolded, "Johnny, how many times do I have to tell you, don't go near the curb!" With tears in his eyes, the frightened little guy replied, "Mommy, what's a curb?"

I once bought a parakeet and promptly started the arduous process of teaching it to talk. "Danny, Danny," I repeated over and over again—fifty repetitions a day for two straight months! I had given up when it finally happened. I was leaving the room and the parakeet blurted out, "Danny, Danny." Not one to stop at my first success, I decided to teach him his last name. "Clark, Clark," I said. This time it only took two hundred repetitions before the bird finally said, "Clark, Clark."

Then something very interesting happened. I got sick and spent two days in the house coughing. When I had recovered, I threw a party for some close friends. As I showed off my talking bird, I discovered a great principle about the education process. I put the bird on my finger and, with a little prompting, it said, "Danny Clark." Then, to everyone's amusement the bird coughed. Of course I didn't teach the bird to cough; he had picked it up the two days I was sick. But it did prove that even a bird is a product of its environment. So are human beings. What goes into our minds will eventually come out.

If you grew up with some bad habits, don't be upset at the people who raised you. Just learn this lesson: if you are one way, you can change. You can be different. You can be any which way you want. Just alter your negative environment and hang in there until you get the desired result. Remember, it's not what's on the outside that matters. Birds communicate with birds, dogs with dogs, people with people, and, most interesting to me, people with birds and dogs and circus elephants and lions and tigers! The Horse Whisperer communicates with horses, and the trainers at Sea World communicate with dolphins and the killer whale Shamu!

Verbal and nonverbal signs, signals, sounds, body language, voice inflections, eye contact, and hand gestures—they are all forms of communication. Humans even have a deeper form of communicating I call the Language of the Heart. I wrote about it in one of my songs:

Language of the Heart
There's a secret language only lovers know
Following their hearts to places heads can never go
Without a word their lips and hands and want-me-eyes reveal
Like dancing partners sensing where to go, they move by feel

Yes the eyes are the window to the soul
Lovers look inside and see that passion makes them whole
Lustfully they fantasize about how love should be
Then find a soul mate seeking self-fulfilling prophecy

Language of the heart is never said or written down
Words can't capture what we mean, the silence makes the sound
Spirit talks to spirit through emotions set apart
The language only lovers know, the language of the heart

There's a secret language only lovers know
Feeling, self-revealing, laying low, and goin' slow
Hearing, tasting, smelling, touching, seeing senses flow
Body talk connecting, only honesty can show

A squeezing one, two, three says I love you
A nod and sultry smile says I am thinking 'bout you too
Touching toes beneath the table is better than dessert
And without public affection is the way real lovers flirt

A tender touch says more than words can say
A kiss heals hurt and sends the pain away
Holding me, like you'll never let me go
Is the reason why I know . . .

Does It Show in Your Face?

Because people who are frequently asked to speak are always in search of new material, quotable quotes, and interesting, off-the-wall facts that make their speeches memorable, let me share some more of my creations and tidbits of info to better illustrate this art of verbal and nonverbal communication:

Does It Show in Your Face?
You don't have to tell how you live each day
You don't have to say if you work or play
A tried, true barometer serves in this place
However, you live, it will show in your face.

The deceit that you bear in your heart
Will not stay inside when it first gets a start
For sinew and blood are a thin veil of lace
What you wear in your heart you wear on your face.

If your life is unselfish, if for others you live
For not what you get, but how much you give
If you live close to God in his infinite grace
You don't have to tell it, it shows in your face.

Truthful Connection

What we've been in the past does not make us who we are today. What we hope to become in the future does. When written language was invented, a critic said, "The discovery of the alphabet will create forgetfulness in learners' souls, because they will not use their memories. They will trust to the external written characters and not remember of themselves." The critic's name was Socrates. Thanks to writing, we still remember much of what he said so long ago. Centuries later, Gutenberg invented printing. Critics said the same thing about print technology. A priest named John Trithemius said printing would weaken the gift of memory so people would forget the vital words they memorized in church. Instead, printing has expanded our memories. Gutenberg's first printed book, the Bible, has been read and remembered more than any other in history. When television arrived, critics said we would stop reading. In fact, television stimulated reading. We publish more books, sell more books, and read more books than ever before. And we know more about what's happening throughout the world than ever before.

Now the "information superhighway" has arrived. It can provide instant access to all knowledge, everywhere. Critics say the human mind can't handle it—the World Wide Web is too much. We'll lose our ability to remember and think. Will the critics be wrong once again? As in the past, new information technologies will expand the human mind, improve learning skills, and make life better than it was yesterday.

Quotable Truth?

For this reason we must make sure our communication is correct, accurate, quotable truth. You see, things aren't always what they seem to be. Perception isn't always reality. It should be, but it isn't. Too many people are outdoing by overdoing and in the process, eventually redoing reality.

When Emmanuel Leutze painted *Washington Crossing the Delaware*, he depicted the Stars and Stripes being carried in the boat, even though it was not adopted as the American flag until June 14, 1777—six months after Washington crossed the Delaware! In his renowned oil painting *Israelites Gather Manna in the Wilderness*, Tintoretto armed Moses's men with shotguns. The earliest known appearance of a gun was approximately 1326—somewhat after the Exodus! In the biography *Abraham Lincoln: The Prairie Years*, Carl Sandburg wrote about Lincoln's mother singing "Greenland's Icy Mountain" as she stood at the family's log cabin door. Quite a feat considering the song was not written until twenty-two years after Lincoln's death!

No wonder life seems so complicated. We bring it upon ourselves. Analyze a bank for instance. It's an institution where you can borrow money only if you present sufficient evidence that you don't need it. What about the American voter who yells at the government to balance the budget and then borrows fifty dollars "just until payday"? What about the father who cheats on his income taxes, yet can't understand why his son cheated on his math test? What about the mother who, while in the midst of lecturing her daughter about always being honest, hears the telephone ring and says, "Tell them I'm not here"? It's true. Things aren't always what they should be. A firefly is actually a beetle—and if we have a bug called a fly, why not a walk or a jog? A Douglas fir tree is actually a pine. An English horn is actually an alto oboe from France. A piece of catgut is actually made from the intestines of sheep. A Turkish bath is actually Roman.

The other day even a reputable radio program threw me for a loop when the disc jockey said, "Now for a partial score—Chicago, seven." Those whom we expect will know what they are doing often don't. The United States Naval Academy of Design held an art competition and awarded second place to a work by Edward Dickenson. The judges later learned that the award-winning piece had been hanging upside down! At the signing of the Treaty of Versailles in 1919, David Lloyd-George of Great Britain advised the leader of Italy that his country could make up its commercial losses by increasing the production of its banana crop. This pronouncement neither heartened nor excited the man since Italy does not produce bananas!

Today's world is even stranger: a woman pays fifty dollars for a beautiful lace slip and gets annoyed if it shows beneath her dress and a man puts up screens to keep insects out of his home and air conditions his house, car, and office, then attends an outdoor picnic! Let us stop the absurd madness of trying to be so sophisticated, complicated, and grandiose. Simple, straightforward connection should be the required standard for all human interactions. It's the only way we will ever align our perception with reality. When we "tell it like it is," not only do we enjoy honest communication, but we also may find that our conversations are entertaining and unobtrusively funny!

When my son was five years old, his mother woke him up for the second day of kindergarten. He snapped, "What, again?" When asked what hitting advice he gives to player Ken Griffey Jr., the batting instructor replied, "I tell him, 'Attaway, Junior!' "

The Power of Humor

Stereotypically, public speakers should avoid talking about religion and politics; however, when tastefully done, a true pro can mix the two to establish him or herself as a bold, straightforward speaker. One of my favorite examples is: President Bush and his secret service are walking through a building when they see an old man with a beard and walking stick, wearing a robe and sandals. President Bush immediately sends over one of his men to speak to the man. "Excuse me, President Bush wants to know if you're Moses." The old man lowers his head and doesn't say a word. Again, the agent asks, "Sir, the president wants to know if you are Moses." Again the old man says nothing. Frustrated, President Bush walks over himself and asks, "Are you Moses?" This time, the old man turns his back and walks away. President Bush and his entourage storm off. Seeing what happened, a curious bystander approaches the old man and asks the same question, "Are you Moses?" This time the old man answers, "Yes, I am." The bystander asks, "Then why didn't you acknowledge that to the president?" Moses answers, "Because the last time I talked to a bush, I ended up wandering in the wilderness for forty years and leading my people to the only place in the Middle East that doesn't have any oil!"

The Power of Words

If plants grow from sunlight, people grow from praise. So give it freely; it costs nothing, and it's so nourishing. Giving compliments always comes back to you—in one form or another. If you give it, you'll receive it, and everybody likes to hear they've done a job well. Put this theory to the test. Start fertilizing your social circle with some recognition and accolades. You'll see the difference soon enough.

The need for praise is basic to everyone. When we receive it, we grow; without it, we shrink and fade. Look for an occasion to give an encouraging word or a compliment. Constantly strive to make people feel wanted and important and capable. Let them know they can succeed. By doing this, we are forced to concentrate on the positive side of people, instead of the negative. This makes us all more productive and pleasant to be around. In sales we call it psychological reciprocity, which simply means this: In the course of our conversation, if I make you feel intelligent, significant, special, and important, it automatically creates a subconscious moral obligation for you to make me feel equally intelligent, significant, special, and important before the conversation ends. It's true. What goes around comes around. "Do unto others as you would have others do unto you" is a pretty general statement.

A note on my mother's refrigerator door served up a deeper explanation.

The Golden Goodies

If you open it, close it.
If you turn it on, turn it off.
If you unlock it, lock it up.
If you break it, admit it.
If you can't fix it, call someone who can.
If you borrow it, return it.

If you value it, take care of it.
If you make a mess, clean it up.
If you move it, put it back.

If it belongs to someone else, get permission to use it.
If you don't know how to operate it, leave it alone.
If it's none of your business, don't ask questions.

If it will brighten someone's day, say it!
If what you have to say will hurt someone, don't say it!
If something isn't broken, don't try to fix it.

It's unbelievable the number of hit shows being patterned after an old formula called a soap opera. In the early days of television they were called soap operas because the shows were sponsored by soap companies. These programs seem to have recurrent themes, and one of them is the character who is always out to ruin the lives of others. He or she creates slander and gossip. These people are insecure and miserable and want those around them to feel the same way.

Wreckers
I watched them tearing a building down
A gang of men in a busy town
With a ho-heave-ho and a lusty yell
They swung a beam and the side wall fell.
I asked the foreman, "Are these men skilled
And the men you'd hire if you had to build?"

He gave a laugh, said, "No indeed!
Just common labor is all I need."
I can easily wreck in a day or two
What builders have taken a year to do
I thought to myself as I went my way
Which of these roles have I tried to play?

Am I a builder who works with care
Measuring life by the rule and square?
Am I shaping my deeds to a well-made plan,
Patiently doing the best I can?
Or am I a wrecker, who walks the town,
Content with the business of tearing down?

The average human brain has unlimited potential. To help us understand the importance of positive thinking, let's look at hypnotism. Any of you who have seen a hypnotist at work will surely agree they are amazing. But hypnotism is nothing more than blind trust. Using concentration, the hypnotist suggests to the mind of the person being hypnotized, and those hypnotized do whatever they are asked to do.

Power of the Mind

The hypnotist tells a shy, timid introvert that she is an exceptional orator, a great entertainer, and a comedian. Incredibly, this quiet, intimidated soul is suddenly transformed into an extroverted speaker who cannot shut up. She says more in five minutes than she has all year. The hypnotist helped the girl overcome her negative feelings about herself by suggesting a positive thought, which the girl accepted as truth. The positive thought replaced the negative, and she responded accordingly.

A friend of mine had trouble with math. Yet under hypnosis he became a math whiz in a matter of seconds. How? Did the hypnotist give him a crash course in mathematics? No. The hypnotist simply told him he could do it. He broke down my friend's self-constructed barrier—the one that had been holding him back from his innate, and previously suppressed, potential.

Two strong football buddies are made into weaklings. Normally they can lift hundreds of pounds, but because of a negative mind-set they cannot even lift a rubber ball or a three-ounce shoe off the table. The mind controls our muscles. When the brain says it can't do something, it really can't. Yet the reverse is also true. When the brain says it can, it really can. These hypnotic demonstrations simply show that we can do anything we make up our minds to do. We have the potential to do the impossible if we firmly believe that we can. Remember, the hypnotist didn't change the strength, knowledge, or experience of the participants. All he did was make suggestions.

Each of us is also hypnotized in a very real sense. As though we are under a hypnotic spell, we do only what we tell ourselves we can do. Therefore, if you're negative, introverted, uncoordinated, weak, stupid, or slow, it's because you tell yourself you are. And because it's up to you, you can change!

When we support good, clean, pure, powerful, and positive elements in life, we become fully charged. We should genuinely care about our neighborhoods and the people who live there. And we should make a stand against those things in our society that are indecent, immoral, and promote violence. In Philadelphia, a woman disguised as a man shot twenty-one bullets into a parked car where a second woman, who was eight months pregnant, waited for her husband. Miraculously, neither the woman nor the baby died. Police identified the shooter and arrested her. When they searched her apartment, they found a library of do-it-yourself crime books, including *The Anarchist Cookbook, How to Disappear Completely and Never Be Found, The Homemade Mortar Construction Manual,* and *Kill Without Joy: The Complete How-to-Kill Book.* One book told how to wear oversized shoes and ankle weights to disguise footprints.

Perhaps we should not be surprised that such how-to books are on the market. Our cherished principle of free speech makes it impossible to censor them. But it takes a sick mind to write, print, buy, and read such books. Every book is a collaborative effort. The author must find a publisher. Retailers must stock the book. Along the way to the bookshelves, dozens of individuals have the opportunity to say, "I won't have anything to do with a book like this." Instead, they supplement the madness of the author with a little madness of their own. The Philadelphia shooting was tragic, but the abuse of freedom that contributed to that shooting was more tragic still.

Robert Redford is a man who believes in taking risks. Someone once asked him about the trappings of fame that go along with being a movie star. Redford replied, "I don't have any illusions of how fleeting fame might be. I constantly remind myself that I only have a few years on earth to say some things. The important thing is to take risks in getting those things said. If you quit taking risks you're liable to lose everything you've worked for."

Again and again, people at the top of their professions are forced to take risks in order to stay there. A researcher named Charles Garfield noticed that many peak performers follow a formula for success. They ask themselves, "Can I survive if the risk I am about to take doesn't work out? Will I be able to go on if I fail?" If the answer is yes—that they could survive the worst possible consequences—then they take the risk. Do they fail? Of course they do sometimes, but they know they will be okay, even if they falter. Self-talk is about creating the right questions. Only when we ask the correct questions can we get the correct answers and solutions, which are the decision-making tools necessary for taking calculated risks. To become successful at whatever we do, we have to take chances. Sure, it's scary. It takes us out of our comfort zones. But with positive self-talk we can go for it! The people who rise to the top, the cream of the crop, talk the talk, then take the risks and walk the walk to success and achievement. And you can too.

Chapter 2

What Is Language For?

Logic, grammar, and rhetoric are the three arts that deal with excellence in the use of language for the expression of thought and feeling. Being grammatical and logical in our soliloquizing while putting our thoughts and feelings down on paper is all that is required and is often awarded with prestigious "Pulitzer Prizes." However, if we desire to be great and powerful public speakers, we must not merely have these two components in our presentation. In order to win a commitment to the conclusion and sentiment we proposed, we must fully embrace and use rhetoric.

The ancient and honorable art of rhetoric is the art of persuasion. To be an amazing public speaker requires both substance and style. Many take courses in public speaking, but most have not been trained in the skills of persuasion. The teaching of rhetoric has usually been about oration and style—style in the use of language and style that makes the communication of substance either more elegant or more effective in both the written and spoken word. However, it is critical to realize that elegance in weaving a tapestry of words may be a desired and mesmerizing bit of sizzle, but it will never compare in effectiveness and long-term impact with passionate persuasion.

The words *oratory* and *rhetoric* are not the same. Oratory is equated with the political platform, the court room, or the legislative assembly. Rhetoric is different, and for the definition we turn to the Greeks and Aristotle in his famous essay, "Rhetoric." Aristotle pointed out the three main tactics to be employed if one wished to succeed in the art of persuasion. The Greeks call these three instruments of persuasion Ethos, Pathos, and Logos.

ETHOS, PATHOS, LOGOS

To address once and for all the most used and obvious diagram of a speech, let me kill two birds here with one stone. Yes, we will clearly and deeply define these Greek descriptions in a moment, but let me quickly put your mind at ease with the simple version: Ethos, Pathos, and Logos represent the beginning, middle, and end of a good speech.

Every great speech has an attention-grabbing opening, at least one middle qualifier, and a memorable close. From a humorous perspective, here are three of my favorites:

1. When they were trying to find someone to give this speech, they phoned the best looking, most dashing, debonair man they knew. He turned them down. So they phoned the most intelligent, educated, brilliant genius they knew. He turned them down, too. So, they asked the sweetest, most humble, sincere guy they had ever met. Hey, I couldn't turn them down three times in a row, so here I am!
2. I heard a speaker once say, "We become what we think about." This is not true. If it were true, I would have been a woman by the time I was twelve years old!
3. I challenge you to drink, steal, swear, and lie. Drink from the fountain of truth, knowledge, and wisdom. Steal a little time each day to do something special for someone when you know you won't get the credit. Swear to make this the best day of your life so far. It may be your last. When you lie down tonight, thank God above that you are free and have the ability to dream mighty dreams and make them come true!

ETHOS

On a serious note, Ethos signifies a person's character. Establishing your character is the preliminary step in any attempt at persuasion. Ethos means others listen to you because they sense that what you have to say is worth listening to. They sense you can be trusted for your honesty and good will and know what you are talking about. Of the three factors of persuasion, Ethos should always come first. Unless you have established your credibility as a speaker and made yourself attractive to your listeners, you will not sustain their attention, much less inspire them to do anything.

Pathos

Whereas Ethos consists in the establishment of the speaker's credibility and credentials (his or her respectable and admirable character), Pathos consists in arousing the passions of the listeners, getting their emotions running in the direction of the action to be taken. Pathos is the motivating factor.

Logos

Logos is the marshalling of reason and must come last. In speaking, it does you no good to give reasons and arguments until you have first established an emotional mood that is receptive to them. In other words, it is critical to first arouse favorable feelings toward your own person and feelings in favor of the end result you are seeking before you can reinforce the feelings with your list of whys. Reasons and arguments have no force unless your listeners are already disposed emotionally to move in the direction that your reasons justify.

All in all, Ethos epitomizes the reasons. Logos is the action to be taken by your listeners, and it confirms the feelings. Pathos is what you have already aroused. With Ethos and Pathos fully operative, Logos remains the winning trump card in the persuader's hand.

For the record, I share all of this to build my credibility as one who researches before I think and thinks before I put anything in a speech. I also lay this foundation that I may demonstrate the importance of engaging both the left brain and the right brain in order to be a most effective public communicator. So far, and ironically, I have engaged your cognitive left brain to explain right brain persuasion. And yes, the profession of public speaking for me is about polishing and perfecting the art of persuasion. However, before we spend the rest of this book and the remainder of the twelve questions dissecting persuasive speaking, let me draw a contrasting speaking purpose.

Persuasion vs. Instruction / Speech vs. Lecture

At the end of the day there are really only two types of speeches: Persuasive Sales and Instructive Education. Though both forms of presentation (written and spoken) consist in telling—and telling is always teaching—the difference between the emotion of sales talk, the non-emotional lecture, and other forms of instructive speech is that one aims at affecting the action or feelings of the listeners, while the other aims at affecting their minds. Both involve persuasion, but for a different purpose.

In the original meaning of the term "lecture," the lecturer was first of all a reader. Today, lecturing is still an oral or spoken presentation closely associated with writing out a speech and then reading it aloud. Some think they are speakers when they use PowerPoint slides, but in reality they are presenters (which we will define in an upcoming chapter) following a previously written-out script. The major challenge in being a lecturer, or what I will hereafter refer to as a presenter, is that the ability to write effectively does not always go hand in hand with the ability to speak effectively. In fact, the contrary occurs more often than not.

Bottom line? Lecturers are presenters of information that instructs. It's the educator teaching math, the accountant explaining your taxes, the boring college professor whipping off Plan A with no voice inflection, or a military officer giving a briefing at a staff meeting for the sole purpose of imparting knowledge. Having said this, I believe that it is a direct violation of our responsibility and a blatant adulteration of the privilege of the platform if we are given an opportunity to speak and all we do is lecture in an instructive presentation. Print out your written essay and email it out. Don't waste our time reading or presenting something we can read for ourselves. Public speaking—in any location, for any reason, to any group—is to instruct and inform, but unless we are moved emotionally to take some kind of action after our time together is over, then our time together was a waste of time! Every presenter can become a speaker if they embrace Ethos, Pathos, Logos, persuasion, and instruction!

For this reason, whenever we are invited to speak, we should "seek to bless, not impress." Listeners should leave you not impressed with you and your achievements, but impressed with themselves and how much they have learned. They should leave you with a belief that if put in the same situation, they too could have done what you did and accomplish what you have done.

Invite the Audience into the Story

When sixteen-year-old Mary Lou Retton scored the perfect ten as a gymnast on the final vault competition in the 1984 Olympics, she became an instant celebrity. I shared the speaking platform with her shortly thereafter. After she delivered her wonderful speech, composed entirely of the excitement and unbelievable achievement of that moment, we chatted. When she asked me for any pointers to improve her presentation, I simply suggested that if she wanted to take her message from wonderful and exciting "look what I have done" to powerful, life changing, and deeply inspiring "you can do it too," what Mary Lou needed to do was share how many times she crashed and burned and wanted to quit gymnastics. What we really wanted to know was about her "ordinary" and the why, how, and when she turned it into "extraordinary."

I'm sure when Mary Lou was learning and practicing her routines that she flew off the bars time after time. She probably fell until her toes bled and the tears streamed down her face. My questions to the audience are: What if Mary Lou had quit after the first ten crashes, never realizing that she was just a few crashes away from success? How many of us would have quit on the fifth or ninth attempt, saying, "I did my best—no one can expect any more?"

It is places like this in the speech where we can insert quotes from famous people to spruce up and validate our reasoning. For example, when England was under attack from the Nazis in World War II and the British needed to rally the people, Winston Churchill said, "It is not enough to say I will do my best. We must do that which is necessary to succeed."

Chapter 3

What Is the Perception?

People don't really care how much we know or what we have done. They only care about what they can learn from what we have learned. They want to be reminded that in life there are no mistakes, only lessons, that pain is a signal to grow, not to suffer. Consequently, people don't relate to our perfections; they relate to our imperfections. Most don't want to hear about our successes; they want to know if we ever failed or fell down and what we did to get back up and try again. If you think about it, when we turn on the news, we don't remember the facts and figures; we remember the interpretation of the facts and figures. We want to know how this information relates to us and our lives.

Satisfying Audience Needs

In Maslow's hierarchy of human needs theory, Maslow suggests that certain needs take precedence over others. Physical needs are the most basic foundational needs because when neglected, they make responding to our other needs difficult. After we satisfy our physical needs, Maslow claims, Safety is critical, followed by feelings of Belonging and that we are Loved. How these needs are satisfied before the meeting begins and how they are sustained throughout the presentation are both extremely important to the success of the speaker.

Physical needs include food, shelter, touch, and water. Hungry people whose stomachs are growling don't concentrate well and really don't give a rat's-wa-kazoodle about building their positive self-esteem until they eat. Being thirsty isn't always a challenge before or during a meeting. However, coffee and juices with breakfast and soft drinks during breaks are important, not only for energy and refreshment, but also because they affect the amount of time a meeting-goer can sit before taking a restroom break. Smokers need their breaks, and smoking a cigarette takes approximately eight minutes.

All of this suggests that the ideal break should be fifteen minutes long. Any longer allows the emotion and momentum you have created to diminish and weaken. The purpose of a break is to let the people take care of their *physical* needs, not check email or return calls. The most effective meetings are those that keep people focused on the theme, message, and purpose in a continuous emotional, intellectual way without distractions so that they experience something they cannot get at home or work.

When an audience is hungry or sitting too long, it is difficult to motivate them to follow your inspirational advice. They are motivated to stretch their legs, go to the snack shack, relieve their bladder, get a drink, or satisfy a real nicotine need. A "presenter" merely shows up and takes the microphone to whip off their "Speech A." A "professional speaker" communicates with the meeting planner ahead of time about where he will be on the program and what happens on the program before he is introduced. The true professional speaker suggests having a break right before he speaks if the audience has been sitting for more than sixty minutes.

In the meeting environment, the physical need for safety is obvious. However, to a professional speaker, safety is about creating a "Safe Environment," where the audience can openly talk about sensitive topics, where men don't feel weak or uncomfortable crying in public, where they can laugh and perhaps sing or jump or stand on our chairs and not feel stupid, and where they can feel safe to be real and in-the-moment, without inhibition.

In this vein, Safety meshes with Belonging and Love. Satisfying these needs is extremely important to a professional speaker. We all need to feel connected to others. We need affection, caring, inclusion, and relationships that make us feel like we fit in. This desire to be included and to be a part of something bigger than oneself is one of the most potent needs that a motivational speaker can utilize in reaching his audience.

Other approaches to fulfilling this need could include describing in your speech the admirable qualities you found in the group, such as the praiseworthy values, charitable natures, and other things that make them proud to be identified as part of the group.

The temperature of the room and the number of people that fit into the space of the room (crammed or roomy) also contribute to satisfying the audience's shelter needs. Trying to connect with and inspire a group that is sweltering from the heat or shivering with cold is an unnecessary and difficult burden to place on a speaker. When the seats are comfortable, the sound system is clear and at the appropriate volume, and the lighting evokes the ambience required for the theme, purpose, and message, then the motivational, persuasive professional speaker doesn't have to fight an uphill battle. He then has the perfect setting to turn attendees into listeners, make them feel loved and that they belong, and change their world one story at a time!

Room Set-Up and Critical Mass

As strange as it sounds, the way in which a room is set up directly influences the way the depth to which a speaker can connect with his audience. Chairs too far from the stage with the front row beginning out of the "intimate zone" or too many chairs and not enough people both disconnect the speaker from audience. Because laughter and emotion are contagious, there is a critical mass necessary for a group to catch the fire of your speech.

Even in a very large room, if you can bunch the smaller group of people together, then you can get a powerful group effect that will help you reach the listeners. Having open seats between the audience members or vacant rows in front of them disrupts the fluid flow of emotion from stage to convention floor and allows the laughter, tears, and inspirational message to weaken before it reaches each listener. Too much space between them will drain that energy away before the group effect can work at all.

Suggestion: Get to the room early for your sound check and use this time to suggest to the meeting planner that the back rows be taped or roped off like construction sites to make people move forward and fill up the room from front to back instead of the usual vice versa. If the room is set for five hundred and only one hundred fifty show up, they and your message are lost in that space. When more people come in late, it prevents you and your listeners from being disrupted as the latecomers fill in the back rows instead of the front rows. If all attendees come, take down the tape or rope and open the rear section.

On one occasion, when I was the second general session speaker at the Arkansas Bankers Association convention, I witnessed a clever way to better control meeting room space. I attended the first session so that I could tie in my remarks to the first presentation. The audience came early to get a back row seat and the room quickly filled up, with every chair and row occupied from the rear forward, up to about the eighth row. As the emcee concluded the introduction of the speaker from the empty front of the room, the speaker had his wireless microphone turned on and immediately started talking in the back of the room. As the listeners cranked their heads around to see the speaker, he simply said, "Isn't it typical for all of us to sit in the back of our meetings so we can feel more casual and sleep or leave if the presenter is boring? Well, well, well. If I could ask each of you to turn your chairs around . . . this is now the new front of the room. And (pointing to the folks five feet in front of him) this is the new front row!" Brilliant!

Instead of struggling to bridge the gap between him onstage and the audience eight rows back, this speaker took control of the situation and, as a true professional, didn't let any distractions alter the powerful impact he was committed to make!

Chapter 4

Do You Get Nervous?

Experts remind us, "If we are prepared, we shall not fear." Fear has been defined as False Evidence Appearing Real. I agree. So it baffles me that experts also tell us that people's number one fear is speaking in public. Ahead of death, spiders, snakes, and the rest of the top ten, standing up in front of people and delivering a speech is the scariest thing we can do? I don't think so.

My greatest fear is the fear of failing—but "proper prior planning and perfect practice prevent poor performance." Preparing ourselves to speak and then preparing the speech eliminates fear. We have gone full circle. Getting nervous is described as "getting butterflies." Preparation gets our butterflies to fly in formation. Nervous energy properly directed is an adrenalin shot that brings us to life onstage. Being nervous keeps us from ever becoming complacent and taking our speaking responsibility lightly. Being nervous before any big event is good, not bad, and in reality is really nothing more than anticipation, excitement, and internal validation that we are finally ready to test our preparation and display our practiced execution.

I've been there, and there is nothing more exhilarating than standing on the five-yard line in a huge football stadium packed full of sixty thousand screaming fans, waiting for the opening kickoff with nervous energy, focusing on what I'm going to do with the ball when it is kicked to me! I experience this same feeling every time the emcee of a meeting begins introducing me to speak. For me, taking the stage and grabbing the microphone is catching the kickoff, running with the ball, and by the end of my speech, scoring a touchdown to win the game!

One humorous experience puts into perspective the perils of perception: I flew into Dallas, Texas, to speak at the convention center. I spent the night at the Hyatt Hotel at the DFW airport. It had been arranged that the husband of the meeting planner would pick me up the next morning and take me downtown for my speech. That night the hotel restaurant had an all-you-can-eat seafood buffet. I must have eaten at least fifty shrimp and clams before turning in. In the middle of the night I woke up with food poisoning. Now, I'm not talking a few stomach cramps here. I'm telling you, I was having labor pains! It felt like somebody had kicked me in the groin and then grabbed my bottom lip and pulled it up over my head! Not only did I throw up all the seafood, but I swear I popped out some Hot Tamales and Red Vines I had eaten in the ninth grade!

With no sleep, my wake-up call alerted me to shave, shower, and put on my suit and tie. I wandered through the restaurant on my way to the lobby, downed two pieces of toast and a handful of soda crackers (trying to settle my stomach), and walked outside to greet my ride. He was in his airline captain's uniform, standing at attention, and in a military, matter-of-fact voice asked, "Are you Mr. Clark?" I acknowledged, got in his car, and we proceeded on our way.

DFW airport is one of the largest airports in the United States and it takes thirty minutes just to get off the premises. Within five minutes of beginning our drive, I quietly asked, "Could you please pull over?" The captain had not said one word to me up to this point, and because I was so weak, I hadn't pushed for conversation either. He said, "What? Right here?" Fighting back a dry heave I blurted, "Yes, now." He slowly put on his blinker and pulled over. I opened the door and totally lost it: "Ralph! Joy! Wha, yaa, ha!" I wiped my mouth clean, closed the car door, and sat up straight. He drove on. Ten minutes later, still without a word from the captain, I burped, "Can you stop again?" This time he jerked the wheel to the right and in a 3-g turn he pulled over and slammed on the brakes. Again I opened the door, hung out of the car, and called for Ralph and Joy again. When I shut the door, he had both hands on the wheel and was sternly staring straight ahead. He sped the rest of the way to the airport exit.

We finally arrived at the convention center but couldn't find a parking spot close to the front entrance. I don't know why the captain didn't just drop me off. Maybe he thought he shouldn't leave me alone, or maybe he thought he should talk to his wife before she met me. In any case, we parked forever away and started to walk. At one hundred degrees with 90 percent humidity and me sporting a dark suit and tie, it only took a few seconds for me to hang a left and sprint to a fence where I could pop my cookies without hitting a car. Wiping my chin for the third time, I rejoined my escort for the grand entrance into the convention center.

As we got to the door, the stoic captain finally broke his silence. "Mr. Clark, may I ask you a personal question?"

I whispered, "Yes."

He asked, "Do you always get this nervous before you speak?"

Chapter 5

What Is the Reality?

There is a difference between being a professional speaker and a professional presenter. A professional speaker spends less time preparing a speech and more time preparing himself to speak. A professional presenter gets his credibility from the speech content and slick delivery. It is memorized and presented with the attitude that it's easier to change the audience than it is to change the speech. Consequently, a professional presenter thinks the time in front of his audience is about him instead of about them. Conversations between professional presenters usually include confessions like, "Wow, the audience loved me on Friday. But on Tuesday, at my other meeting, they were stupid—didn't get half my jokes or relate to me at all."

How shallow is this? It's like showing up to a dinner party and pulling out three by five cards with your conversation written out on them and engaging the people at your table only in a planned, practiced, nonspontaneous way, void of sincerity, two-way nonverbal communication, and authentic connection. The only place from which a person can grow is where he is. You must follow your audience physically and emotionally. Only there can you gently invite them to buy into your message. It is the secret to sales, customer service, coaching, parenting, human resource management, leadership, teaching, and public speaking. Because of this, the purpose of a meeting is to take the audience members on an emotional, thought-provoking roller coaster ride to a higher place than they can take themselves and to give them a deeper experience than they can get at home or work. How dare anyone, especially a professional presenter, adulterate their opportunity to touch someone's life by taking their privilege of the platform so lightly? If the presentation is about PowerPoint illustrations, videos, graphs, or information, doesn't it seem completely ridiculous to bring people together at great travel and time expense just to have someone stand up in front of them to rattle off some cookie-cutter presentation that could have been emailed to everyone individually?

Professional presenters tell, teach, and coach other wannabe professional presenters to find the person in the audience who is smiling and nodding in total agreement and then to feed off that person throughout their entire speech. No, no, no! These are the folks who also tell you to come from backstage when you are introduced. Again, no. Always sit in the back of the room to get a reality check on the emotional state of those who don't want to be there.

When you are introduced, you have ample time to get to the stage. Then, when onstage, immediately start looking for the youngest and oldest male and female and the most negative male and female who disagree with you. The challenge and reward of your speech then becomes to relate to each of them, to truly connect and positively touch their lives, knowing that if they get it, everyone else has as well.

PREPARING YOURSELF TO SPEAK

Don't trust your memory. When you hear an extraordinary joke, immediately write it down. Always carry a small, pocket-sized notebook around with you. You never know when you're going to see or hear a powerful quotable quote, hear something funny, witness a unique metaphor or analogy for successful living, or participate in a significant emotional experience—you can't afford to forget the intimate details that touched your soul forever.

Why my emphasis on extraordinary belly-aching jokes, powerful perfectly worded quotable quotes, and eyewitness personal accounts? Because these are the key ingredients of an extraordinary, entertaining, thought-provoking, unique, inspirational speech that allow you to speak with authority. Being able to share your own observations, analogies, and life-changing experiences is what turns a professional presenter into a professional speaker and puts you in demand.

Finding and developing your own stories comes through simple self-audited, self-administered question and answer sessions. Some ideas include thinking about your first job interview, first date, being fired, parenting, traffic tickets, vacation or travel screw-ups, embarrassing moments, family holidays, changing your first diaper, and so forth. With passion, creativity, and imagination, the sky is the limit.

What makes a professional speaker uniquely different and in high demand, and what allows a professional speaker to command a much higher speaker's honorarium than a professional presenter, is not the content and slick delivery of the speech while he is onstage. It is everything he has thought and experienced, and it is the person he has become long before he came onstage. It's being exactly the same offstage as you are onstage.

Speaking professionally is not putting on a show. The speech doesn't give you credibility; your life does! Being a professional speaker is about sharing the hours and years of incredible experiences, responsibilities, failures, and successes that you amassed before you began your speech. And even though you only have a sixty-minute time slot in which to impart your wisdom, your audience sees, feels, and senses your depth, character, and the library of knowledge that is left unspoken.

Professional speakers have so much more to say and give that oftentimes they are invited back to speak to the same audience again. Professional speakers should always come across as the tip of the iceberg—the audience should feel that they have only heard the surface, only 10 percent of the huge, wide, solid iceberg beneath.

Bottom line reality? Every speech should inspire and persuade. This means every informational or educational speech should not be a speech at all. It should be an email, fax, or letter. If you want me to remember facts and figures, you must give them to me in written form so that I can read, ponder, read again, study, and internalize them over time. However, if you want us to improve, increase our productivity, and become more of who we are, then gather us all together that we may see who our leaders are and, in turn, allow them to earn the required respect from us that gives them the right to the title of leader.

Story Power

The greatest compliment anyone can pay me as a professional speaker is to call me a master storyteller. Stories work by connecting concepts and facts with feelings. When you merely mention important ideas to an audience, they may agree with their importance. But not many will remember the specifics because to the audience, they are cold, hard, and distant. You have offered them no personal or intimate reason to remember your points. However, wrap those same concepts in a stimulating, emotional story, and not one of them will forget the story or the ideas associated with it.

Speaker coach Max Dixon gave this advice: "Continue to develop the 'storyness' of your presentation. Share stories of victory and not victimization, suiting length of story to importance of point. A well-crafted, well-told story can create exceptional rapport with any audience, especially if you utilize the emotional power of words to paint pictures: 'a tonic of opportunity,' 'an embracing development,' 'just let that idea relax by the fire until it feels like talking,' and so forth."

In our storytelling we should carefully select words that best shape the space we are describing such as suffocating relationship, intoxicating conversation, claustrophobic cubicle. In a single crafted sentence, the right words can evoke memories and associations with our senses of smell and taste (the very mention of "cinnamon" stimulates a real sensory effect). It can also conjure up vivid images that invite the attendees to actively participate in defining the image you are creating, for instance, "what are *your* sounds of silence?"

The story is the "for instance," or illustrative example, that binds the point with the proof and the idea to the listener's bottom-line belief. Give me an idea—complex or simple, deeply philosophical or cognitively scientific—while you have me laughing or crying, and I will always remember your speech and never forget your lesson!

Real Life Rocky

Sylvester Stallone is the perfect example of someone who looked in their own life for an inspirational story that could help others. Let me share the inspirational story behind the *Rocky* movie series. Stallone, through fate or circumstance, ended up at the Muhammad Ali versus Chuck Wepner heavyweight fight. Wepner, a battling, bruising type of club fighter who had never really made the big time, was now having his shot. But the fight was not regarded as a serious battle. It was called a public joke. He would barely go three rounds, most of the predictions said. Well, the history books will read that he went fifteen rounds and established himself as one of the few men who had ever gone the distance with Muhammad Ali. Stallone later wrote that that night must have meant more to Wepner than any money he could have ever received from fighting because now he had run the complete circle. It was the reason he had been training for thirty-four years.

At that time Sylvester Stallone was a starving "nobody" actor with a dream to write a movie script. That fight was the inspiration for his main character. He was going to create Rocky Balboa, a man from the streets, a walking cliché of sorts, the all-American tragedy, a man who didn't have much mentally but had incredible emotion, patriotism, spirituality, and good nature, even though nature had not been good to him.

With his lead character identified, he then needed a specific story line for the movie, which turned out to be Stallone's own personal story of his inability to be recognized, looking only for a break to show what he could do. So, Stallone took his own predicament and injected it into the character of Rocky because no one, he felt, would be interested in a story about a down-and-out, struggling actor and writer. But Rocky Balboa was different. He was America's child. He was to the seventies what Charlie Chaplin's Little Tramp was to the twenties.

What some do not know is that the catch in Stallone's sales pitch to the film production companies was that Stallone came with the script. If they wanted to make the movie, Sylvester would definitely be playing the lead part and star as Rocky. The rest is history—Academy Award for Best Picture, followed by five sequel *Rocky* movies released in subsequent years with the final *Rocky VI* in 2006 to complete the enormously successful series. In a nutshell, Sylvester Stallone faced his fears and didn't just let life come to him; he came to life. He conceived, he believed, and because he planned his work and worked his plan, he achieved exactly what he set out to do.

Bottom line? This story was there. All Stallone had to do was stop his hectic life long enough to figure out what the story was. You and I can and should do the same! Countless stories occur in our personal and professional lives all around us. We need only find them, define their meaning and purpose, capture them in writing, practice telling them, and add them to our repertoire as speakers.

I did it with my short story "Puppies for Sale," which I wrote in junior high school. It was made into a short film at Paramount Studios starring the late Jack Lemmon and ten-year-old Jesse James. Another story I wrote that same year is called "The Circus," which is a tender "service-before-self" story about my dad and me buying tickets to go to the circus. Both stories have become international favorites in the *Chicken Soup for the Soul* series and came as a result of me looking for the stories going on in my life and figuring out what lessons they taught.

Developing Your Unique Factor

You cannot be an inspirational speaker if what you did that makes you inspirational is yesterday's news. The reason my message is fresh is because I am. I am always creating opportunities to push myself with the belief that no matter what my past has been, I have a spotless future. Your "Unique Factor" is different than your "Signature Story," which is the one Significant Emotional Experience (S.E.E.) in your life that gives you the right to be a professional speaker.

I am talking about always going for the gusto and doing extraordinary things that don't regularly occur in ordinary life. I am talking about reading one book a week for the last thirteen years (I have) and attending special concerts and historic events that will give you experiences to share. I am always looking to develop relationships by giving much more than I take so these relationships can pay off someday if the opportunity presents itself. Because of this mentality, my unique factor in the market is: "I wonder what cool thing Dan has done this year? I wonder what big name celebrity Dan has interviewed this month? I can't wait to have Dan back to demonstrate to our people that we shouldn't let ourselves get stale or stagnant!"

If a person's resume is the same this year as it was last year, shame on that lazy, non-passionate, non-creative, non-imaginative person who is stuck in their past. We must commit to being lifelong learners, to taking calculated risks into areas that teach us things we cannot learn from PowerPoint presentations and books. This is why we need speakers. We must always remember that the purpose of a meeting is to give someone an experience they can't get at home or work and to take them to a place they cannot take themselves. In order to do this, the speaker must have already done it in his own life! Make a list of amazing things you want to do. After you experience each one, it is easy to figure out what you learned from it. This becomes another arrow in your quiver, another club in your golf bag of stories you can choose from to help you customize your remarks.

Make Yourself Fascinating to Listen To

I flew an F-18 fighter jet at twice the speed of sound. The details of my five hours of training and the actual ninety-minute flight are hilarious and extraordinary. At the end of the story the message is contained in this conversation that I had with the pilot.

"How do you fly this high-tech machine?"

The pilot answered, "By feel."

You fly a high performance jet with the right side—the touchy, feely, creative, emotional side of your brain. Then I relate this message to the specific job description of that particular audience and tack on the powerful message of change that I learned in the cockpit. In an F-18, the control stick is straddled between your knees. It moves three inches forward, three inches to the left and right, and five inches backward. You need only move that control stick one inch in either one of those four directions and it completely changes the entire direction of the aircraft forty-five degrees. Message? Small deliberate change makes a huge difference. And now, because of the prior research I did on the organization, I can give them specific examples of small changes they could make as individuals and as an organization.

Staying with this same peak performance flying example, I then take the audience's understanding of "feel" and "the little things really do matter—yes we should sweat the small stuff" to a deeper place by contrasting another fighter jet ride I had with the U.S. Air Force Thunderbirds. We did every air-show maneuver, went mach, and caught 9.4 Gs. The F-16 does not have a floor mounted control stick but rather a control grip mounted on the right side of the cockpit. It is a "fly-by-wire" system where the grip only moves three eighths of an inch. You can't even tell you are moving it. We were airborne for ninety minutes, thirty of which I got to fly. So when we landed, I asked the pilot how we flew this incredible F-16. He said, "You become the plane." He then asked a question that drives home for every audience in every industry the critical importance of taking personal responsibility for our sales calls, our management expectations, and our everyday opportunities to live a lifetime every day. The pilot asked, "When you climbed up the ladder to slide into the cockpit, did you strap yourself into the F-16, or did you strap the F-16 onto you?"

Check out my website at danclarkspeak.com. Who knows? Perhaps I can be a source of inspiration. I have raced automobiles in Germany and dog sleds in the Arctic, ridden camels in Morocco and elephants in Thailand. I was honored to carry the Olympic Torch in the 2002 Winter Olympic Games. I was the emcee on the Kenny Loggins Charity Telethon in Santa Barbara, California, where we raised $752,000 dollars in only twelve hours on the air. Yes, my list goes on and I guarantee it will continue to grow in extraordinary experiences so that I stay exciting and interesting to listen to. Remember, a true professional speaker only uses his own material and the cool, exhilarating, once-in-a-lifetime, right-to-the-edge, pushed-to-the-limit experiences he has had to illustrate his points. What will be your "Unique Factor?"

With all due respect, in 2004 I shared the program with a professional presenter who had climbed Mt. Everest in 1982. He was introduced as an inspirational speaker, but I couldn't help overhearing many of the sophisticated, successful audience members who said, "Cool photos, but what has he done lately?"

Take Relationships to a Deeper Level

The other night I had to take my four-year-old daughter to the hospital. Sitting in the emergency room, I just wanted to fit in and look like and be like everyone else. A macho man came in with his son, and the physician asked about the problem. "My boy fell down and broke his leg. Didn't even cry!"

I thought, *Oh, perfect.*

A mother came in with her little girl. The physician inquired about her daughter. "My daughter fell off the beam at the gymnastics meet and badly twisted her knee."

I thought, *Oh, perfect!*

The doctor finally asked me why I was there with my daughter. I said, "She has a raisin stuck in her nose!"

Everybody laughed. I just wanted to fit in, but my little girl taught me that it's okay to be outside the lines!

A father came home from work and his five-year-old son met him in the driveway. "Daddy, welcome home. Daddy, will you play baseball with me?" His father flippantly responded, "I have too much work to do. I don't have time. But I want you to know that I love you." His little boy replied, "Dad, I don't want you to love me. I want you to play ball with me!"

Take Competition to Its Highest Fulfillment

A young girl with a serious mental handicap ran in the fifty-yard dash competition of the national Special Olympics track and field meet. When she lost the race, she turned to all the timers, track personnel, meet officials, and fellow athletes and taught them all one of the greatest, most profound lessons of competition. With an IQ of forty-two, she said, "I finished at my best, and you have to give it your all and finish best before you can ever finish first!"

Take Mistakes to Their Sweetest Solutions

A little boy spilled cranberry juice on the new carpet in his living room. Shaking with fear and sobbing giant tears of pain, he humbly walked into the kitchen to confess.

"Mom, I'm so sorry. I just spilled my big glass of juice on your new carpet. I feel very, very bad."

His mother hugged him and said, "It's okay. Don't be sad. We can get you another glass of cranberry juice."

Take Work to Its Greatest Enjoyment

As we were coming in for a landing at the Dallas Fort Worth airport, our Delta Airlines jet hit heavy turbulence and bounced all over the sky. When we finally touched down, the flight attendant spoke over the cabin public-address system.

"Welcome to Dallas, Texas. If you enjoyed your flight, tell your friends you flew Delta. If you did not enjoy your flight, tell your friends you flew Southwest."

Take Embarrassment Out of Play

One afternoon at a sales convention, the closing speaker's microphone went out and he yelled, "Some days you're the bug; some days the windshield!" He spoke from the heart for a few minutes and then apologized for having to leave early. He said, "I've got to go. Tonight my wife and I are sharing our wedding anniversary with you. Yep. Me and my wife have enjoyed seventeen great years of marriage—seventeen out of fifty-five ain't bad!"

Take Private Victories Way Beyond Public Victories

At a gala fund-raiser, I was sitting next to the distinguished actor Mr. Gregory Peck. Throughout the evening, every other celebrity had been acknowledged and introduced—all except Mr. Peck. A journalist finally approached him to apologize. He simply replied, "No apology necessary. If you have to tell them that you are, then you aren't."

Support

John McMaster became a superstar basketball player in high school. For each of his three years on the team he was All-Conference, All-State. In his final season he was named the most valuable player of the league. John's mother never missed a game, home or away, regardless of the travel distance or weather conditions. His mom was always in the bleachers cheering her son to victory. Interestingly, John's mother was totally blind! What's the message? Although the mother could not see her son, he could see her. Support makes the special difference!

Chapter 6

How Do You Determine Your Message?

Some things are true whether you believe them or not. Everybody is entitled to their own opinion, but nobody is entitled to the wrong facts. Right is right. Period. There are certain universal, time-tested, natural laws and proven principles that have always been around and that are always at work and always right. Gravity was at work long before the apple conked Newton on the head. You don't win with the best players; you win with the right players. "Best" is comparing yourself to *who* is right and based on competition against others. "Right" is comparing yourself to a higher standard of performance, ethics, core values, and success principles based on *what* is right. Right is truth and is not voted on or made policy because majority rules. Right and truth are correct all by themselves or together in the cosmos.

Why do I bring this up? When anyone asks me to help them become a professional speaker, I always ask them one question: "What would you drive five hours one way to say to someone if it wasn't for a loved one and you were not being paid for your speech?" If their answer is that they wouldn't, then I politely tell them they don't have what it takes to be a professional speaker. One of the things I am most proud of is the fact that over twenty-five years I have missed only one speech. This is over four thousand audiences in all fifty states and thirty-five foreign countries. My missed speech was because I was taken to the emergency room and the doctors wouldn't let me leave the hospital in time to fly cross country.

I've had planes cancel and weather delays and airports close, but I have always scrambled. Many times I have run through airports to catch a different airline just leaving, chartered King Airs and Lear Jets at my own expense, and rented cars to drive several hours just to keep my commitments. My message is clear, and I need to share it with the world.

Signature Story

I played football for thirteen years. One day in practice, the coach had us run into each other full speed—a tackling drill. Lyle's helmet hit my neck and shoulder. My eye drooped, I momentarily lost my speech, my right side went numb, and my right arm dangled at my side. I remained in this paralyzed condition for over a year. Sixteen doctors told me I would never get better. As I worked hard and invented my own combination of physical and emotional therapy, a year later I enjoyed a 95 percent recovery.

As I started to get better, I was asked to speak. This was in 1982. What was my message? You can if you think you can. What did my message evolve into as I drilled deeper into its truth? No matter what our past has been, we have a spotless future; failure is an event, not a person. If we're not failing a few times it means we are not pushing ourselves hard enough. Most people who think they are depressed are not—there is a huge difference between being depressed and being disappointed or discouraged. Fatigue and pain make cowards out of us all.

The only way I was able to fight my way through this paralyzing injury that cut short my football career was to realize the difference between the person and the performance—that football was just what I did, not who I was as a man. I had to comprehend that when we identify ourselves in terms of what we do instead of who we are, we become human doings instead of human beings.

I started to recover only when I stopped focusing on having fame and started focusing on being whole—only when I focused on purposes instead of just setting goals. This was my message at thousands of high schools and colleges to hundreds of thousands of teenagers and young adults. That was then. What about now? In 1991, I made the transition into the corporate arena. Has my message changed? No. My illustrations and depth of understanding have changed, but right and true are still right and true.

I was so down and out, lost, lonely, and confused when I was injured that I almost gave up on life itself. I had plenty of concerned people come up to me and say, "I know what you're going through," but it only angered me because I thought there was no way they could know. I wanted to scream, "No, have someone rip your arm off and break your heart in a million pieces, and take away your lifelong dream to play professional football and walk around paralyzed for a year and then tell me how it feels!" They didn't have a clue what I was going through, which meant they wouldn't know how to help me get better either!

So why have I not missed speeches? Why have I driven five hours one way to speak for free? Because I've been way down, and I honestly believe that I really do know how others feel and that my message will help them heal.

The Use of Music

Frustrated singers and wannabe entertainers should not use the privilege of the platform to impose their unfulfilled dreams on a captive audience. The world of professional speaking has no place for closet karaoke singers. Speakers should never use music in their presentations, especially at the conclusion, in the form of a song unless the music and the message of the music have everything to do with the message of the speech. I often conclude my speeches with a song that I have written and recorded that reinforces my reason for being there. One song I recorded on my first album with a group called Sun, Shade and Rain that I've sung all over the world that was appropriate whenever the requested message for that group was hope, never say never, positive symbolism, death is only a comma not an exclamation point, and the importance of creating a supportive family in both our personal and professional lives is called, "I'll Build You a Rainbow." It's a story that I tell to background music where I only sing the chorus.

I'll Build You a Rainbow

(Chorus)
I'll build you a rainbow, way up high above
Send down a sunbeam, plumb full of love
Sprinkle down raindrops, teardrops of joy
I'll be happy as spring time, watching over my boy

(Narration 1)

Once there was a little boy named Jamie
He had some great friends, but his greatest friend was his mom
She was just different than the other moms

While they were busy going to their fashion shows
And their bridge parties, she was home with him
They'd play in the backyard, go on bike rides, have long talks
She was the greatest football player on the whole block
At least that's what the other guys said
They thought she was really something
And wished their moms could be a lot more like that

(Chorus)
I'll build you a rainbow, way up high above
Send down a sunbeam, plumb full of love
Sprinkle down raindrops, teardrops of joy
I'll be happy as spring time, watching over my boy

(Narration 2)
Then one day Jamie was called home from school
There was a big white ambulance in the driveway
Jamie walked through the front door
And saw his dad talking to the doctor
Jamie was scared
They said he could only talk to his mom for a minute
He tiptoed into the bedroom and saw her lying on the bed
She smiled and whispered, "Hi, Big J."
That's what she always called him, even though he wasn't very big
She said he had a big heart
She said, "Jamie, I'm going away and I won't be coming back, pal,
I'm dying."
Big tears filled Jamie's eyes
"Mom, you just can't die."
She said, "It's okay, Babe, there's no regrets
I've been with you more in eleven years
Than most moms are with their boys in a whole lifetime."
He said, "I know Mom, but you just can't die, you just can't."
She said, "Jamie, there's a secret. And it's a very special secret

I want you to always remember—families are forever
And even though you won't see me, I'll still be there."
"But, Mom, if I can't see you, how will I know that you're there?"
She paused and thought for a minute, and then she smiled and said

(Chorus)
I'll build you a rainbow, way up high above
Send down a sunbeam, plumb full of love
Sprinkle down raindrops, teardrops of joy
I'll be happy as spring time, watching over my boy

(Narration 3)
She kissed him, closed her eyes, and she was gone
Jamie and his Dad stood on the front porch watching the ambulance
Drive away and his Dad broke down and started to cry
They hugged each other real tight and Jamie felt his Dad's tears on
His own cheeks and he cried too
But then he remembered the secret and he looked up
And sure enough, there is was, right over their house
A great big rainbow, just like she promised and he said
"Dad, Dad, it's alright—families are forever!"

(Chorus)
I'll build you a rainbow, way up high above
Send down a sunbeam, plumb full of love
Sprinkle down raindrops, teardrops of joy
I'll be happy as spring time, watching over my boy

Chapter 7

Is Public Speaking a Calling?

When I was paralyzed playing football, the doctors told me I wouldn't recover, but recover I did. As I got better, I was asked to speak. The more I spoke, the more I was asked to speak. Through 100 percent referrals, I parlayed speaking into a full-time profession, averaging over one hundred fifty full-fee speaking engagements annually since 1982.

My point?

I didn't choose speaking as my career; it chose me. Without flattering myself, I had a message and an experience that people wanted to hear about and learn from and the phone just kept ringing. For this reason, I cringe when someone comes to me and says they have decided they want to become a professional speaker. Others may disagree, but I believe professional speaking is not something anyone can choose. Being a professional speaker is a calling.

For some reason, you have been singled out and "knighted" to serve a mission for humanity. Your purpose is larger than making money—you truly believe you are on this earth and have been given certain experiences that you may share with others to help bring peace, goodwill, love, success, and extraordinary achievement to your fellow beings. This is why I ask wannabes, "What is your message?" Not what do they think the market is looking for or what is the current buzz-word, popular topic of the month. What do they know to be true from their own experience that they feel honored, compelled, and committed to share with everyone who will listen?

If you feel you have been "called" to be a professional speaker, here are the three questions you must ask and answer and the one next step you must take to turn your calling into reality: What would you drive five hours one way to say to somebody? What is your specific message? Who would benefit from your message? This identifies your market (students, educators, athletes, sales professionals, customer service agents, military, doctors, government employees, IT). Where does your market meet? This identifies your marketing location (schools, trade association conventions, corporate training meetings, sales rallies). Do what is necessary to get your name and message in front of the decision-makers and get booked on their programs. And the one next step you should take is to join the National Speakers Association and become an active member.

Chapter 8

ARE THERE COMMUNICATION SYSTEMS?

Knowledge + Motivation = Peak Performance

Let me briefly take you into my world and explain this in terms of writing and speaking. Readers and audiences don't care what I've done. They care what I've learned. Even more, they care what they will learn from me. The goal of any book or seminar should be to help others turn success into significance. This is a double-edged sword. First, the author or speaker must prepare and see himself not as a Training Provider but as a Training Adviser. If he is merely writing or presenting, the reader or seminar attendee only becomes impressed with the author or speaker. However, if the book or seminar truly trains and advises, the reader or attendee becomes impressed with himself and closes the book or leaves the seminar as his own motivator. Providers are short-term, opinionated, and accepted. Advisers are long-term, factual, and trusted.

Some leaders or organizations see training as an interruption and cost. Do you? Organizations that are truly in the people-building business, that actually want to win with desired results, have leaders who look at training as an investment. And the Return on Investment (ROI)? Both management and labor become the change they wish to see, and when held accountable, give results not reasons and realize there is no failure, only feedback. And because the investment was not in "providers" but in "advisers," the long term ROI is that everybody in the organization, from the top down and side to side, is committed to execute the following formula on their own and keep the book or seminar relevant and active in both their personal and professional lives.

This formula was developed by my friend and colleague Mr. Bob Pike. I recommend him as one of the premier trainers of trainers, trusted advisers, and success coaches on the planet. He is based out of Minneapolis and can be reached at BobPikeCTT@aol.com. Bob simplifies and quantifies the necessity to blend true facts and inspired feelings. I respectfully refer to this simple, profound equation as Pike's Peak Performance Process.

K + M = PP
(Knowledge plus Motivation equals Peak Performance)

K – M = LEI
(Knowledge minus Motivation equals Less than Expected Improvement)

M – K = EI
(Motivation minus Knowledge equals Energized Incompetence)

Notice that Knowledge *minus* Motivation *disappoints* and Motivation *minus* Knowledge breeds *Mediocrity*. As Mr. Miyagi counseled in the movie *Karate Kid*, "Ambition without knowledge is like a boat on dry land." Obviously, to succeed at anything, and then to take that success to the highest performance level called significance, requires an equal measure of Motivation and Knowledge. One without the other is a waste. I see this truth in certain religions in the world that suggest a once-a-month fast. But fasting without purpose and prayer is just going without food!

I also see this in the speaking profession. Some speakers eloquently "heat up" the audience and give them a rah-rah "sunburn" that is bright red for a few days with excitement, sensitivity, and revitalized resolve. And yes, after a few more days the "burn" fades into a "tan" where they are feeling better and optimistic that they can sustain the new healthy look. But it's only a matter of time before they start to "peel" and the momentary new tan-colored outside reverts back to the old pale "real" beneath it all. As they say, "Motivation without education is frustration—we need a blend of facts and feelings. We always need high touch in a high-tech world!"

Chapter 9

How Do You Use the Systems?

Attention, Hope, Action

As you know, I am a professional speaker. My job is to teach, inspire, guide, push, and pull others to reach their full potential—not to impress, but to bless and take them (and you) to a higher place than they can take themselves. Too many speakers and seminar leaders use "cutesy" shallow gimmicks, telling their listeners to "visualize" what they desire and to put a picture of the cruise ship vacation, sports car, elegant mansion, water ski boat, or whatever their dream may be, up on their refrigerator door. No, no, no!

To get what you want and, more important, become exactly who you want to be, don't visualize or look at the photo of the muscle-bound hunk or perfectly shaped super model. Visualize yourself going to the gym, sweating through the hard times, working out thirty minutes every morning no matter what. Visualize saying no to your second piece of cheesecake. Visualize making five more sales calls per week and coming to work early and staying late. In fact, to get yourself ready to fully embrace this last step-by-step formula, visualize the simple yet profound process that must be experienced before you can really change your life forever, improve yourself, and reduce chance from your everyday experience.

This process has no specific name but was explained to me by my speaker coach, Dr. Blaine Lee, who, among other things, is a national best-selling author of *The Power Principle* and founder of the National Speakers School. According to Dr. Lee, in order for one person to actually influence another to let go of their past, take control of their dreams, and move forward on creating desired alterations in their personal and professional lives, three things must happen.

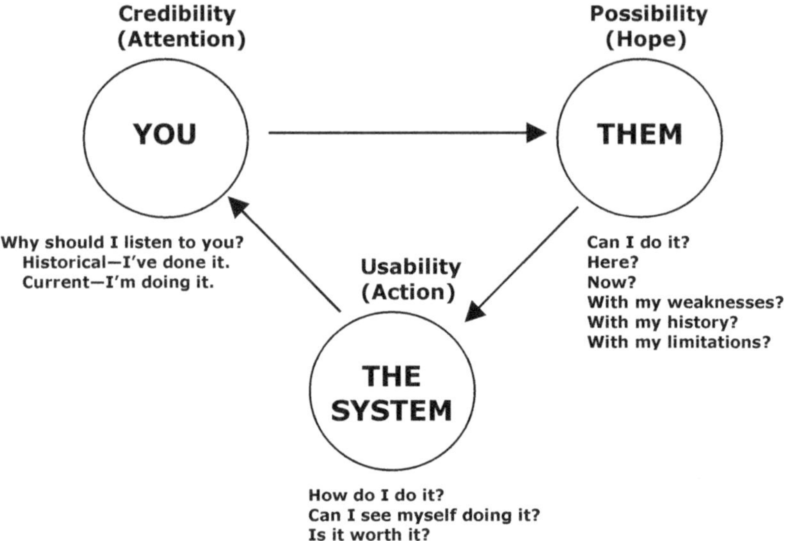

As you can plainly see, the speaker, author, seminar facilitator, life coach, or organizational leader needs to answer the number one question, or there won't be a second one. Every audience member needs and deserves to know: "Why should I listen to you?" The answer builds the necessary credibility to get the listener's, reader's, or employee's attention. Through further illustrations, documented research, and inspirational stories, the speaker can speak with authority and give hope that they can also do what you have done. Only now will they believe strongly enough to take action and use the system in their lives because they know it is worth it.

Chapter 10

How Do You Give an Amazing Interview?

You already know the most important part of the answer. First, you must know what you believe. To get a better answer, you must ask a better question. Ask yourself the easy and especially the tough questions and respond to them honestly and completely. You can fool others for a while, but you can never fool yourself. Therefore, always tell the truth. If and when you tell the truth, you don't have to worry about remembering anything!

Back in the stage of figuring out what you would drive five hours to say to someone for free, you were invited to decide what your personal message is. And if your experiences, discovered meaning, and practical purpose in life invoke a deep conviction that public speaking is a "calling," then responding to someone's questions on or off camera, onstage or offstage, on air or off air, or on the record or off the record is no big deal.

You know what you know; people want to know it and learn from you and, through a question-and-answer process, you tell them. Once you know what your message is, research the topic thoroughly and memorize key facts, quotes from experts, and chapter and verse sources of time-tested data that you can repeat at any time during any interview. The critical point here is that you understand the difference between an interview with you posed as an expert eyewitness "reporter" and you just sharing your "opinion." Either way, you need to know what you're talking about and come across as someone who has spent a great deal of time thinking about this subject.

Five Simple Steps to Giving an Amazing Media Interview

Among the five suggestions, the first two are the most important:

1. Keep every answer to thirty seconds

This is so the interviewer has time to ask you as many questions as possible in the time allocated. This makes the interview flow and keeps it much more interesting. Thirty-second answers must be practiced and rehearsed. As you ask yourself the easy and the toughest questions and give yourself, and perhaps a friend or coach, the long complete answer, continue to practice this process until, through an intense editing process, you finally end up with your concise but conversational thirty-second reply.

2. Take charge

Before the interview begins, decide what specific messages, points of interest, facts, and short stories you definitely need to share. Decide on the specific image you need to convey and what nonverbal elements must be used in order to be judged as you need to be judged, such as hairstyle and length; business or business casual attire; color of shirt, suit, and tie.

Oftentimes you are told the interview will last ten minutes, and when you arrive, they have reduced your time to three minutes. When you already know the most important thing you want to bring up and get out of the interview, this diminishing of your opportunity doesn't stress you out. You simply edit your thoughts and make sure you get to your point immediately. This "getting to your point" and "taking charge of every interview" is different than taking control. The one asking the questions is always in control of the conversation. However, taking charge is knowing what you want to talk about. Therefore, regardless of the question asked, you can turn it into an opportunity to get your point across. In the world of great interview skills it's known as "bridging." When the interviewer throws you a curve question that you either don't want to answer or don't have time to answer if you are to keep to your agenda, the three simplest "bridges" are:

"Before I get to that, let me fill you in . . ."

"Let us consider the larger issue here . . ."

"Instead of that, you should ask me about _____. Let me tell you what happened . . ."

Bridging can get you out of the most difficult situations. Example: OJ Simpson went on trial for the murders of his wife, Nicole, and Ron Goldman. The televised trial started on the first day of camp of the next NFL football season. Reporters were everywhere. I was at the Raiders camp in Oxnard, California, and not one question relevant to football was asked to any player. All the television reporters wanted to know about their personal lives. Microphones were literally stuck in the faces of every prominent athlete with personal inquiries: "How many times have you beat your girlfriend?" "Have you ever abused your wife?" "Did you have an abusive father and come from a dysfunctional family situation?"

Rather than answer these questions, and instead of avoiding the media altogether, a player could have replied with his own platform message, "The real question here is can we leave our work at the office and balance out our lives? All of us men need to make sure our personal relationships with our wife and family are good and positive. And in order to do this we must realize that before we can respect someone else we must first respect ourselves. This is the secret to building a winning family and a winning team, which is the only reason I am at football camp. Like my teammates, I want to get better every day so that, together, we can win the championship this year!"

When Alexander the Great invaded India, he brought before him wise men and asked them a question. To spice things up, he said if they got the answer wrong they would be put to death. Question: "Which is the most cunning of beasts?" The answer they gave, which saved their lives: "That which men has not discovered." Brilliant, eh? The wise men lived.

Bridging gets you from where you are in the conversation to where you would rather be. The best guests don't evade the difficult questions. If you ignore them, they will be asked again. In this case, restructure the question before answering by offering additional information not required by the question. When asked if you support President Bush's policy in Iraq, which is extremely controversial and will immediately divide your listeners into pro and con mode, you would restructure the question: "That is a fascinating question. I think all of us need to ask ourselves about this concept of support. When we say we support the troops, we must ask ourselves what we are supporting. Can we support the troops and not Bush? Do you support the fact that President Bush has appointed more women and more minorities and has given more money for AIDS research and African AIDS relief than any other U.S. president in history? Do you support your Senator, who voted yes on this issue and yet no on these major bills?" Give reliable facts and credible statistics in your new information and they will never come back to the original, difficult, controversial question!

To minimize the hazards of being interviewed, remember three things: be prepared, have conviction, and express your facts and opinions with enthusiasm! If you are not excited about your message, why should anyone else be? Be anecdotal. Use examples and quick, short, powerful stories that the audience will remember.

3. Wardrobe

You are the message, not your clothing. Never wear anything so odd, controversial, or flashy that it draws attention away from you to your outfit.

For men, avoid white shirts and light blue everything. Gray, darker blues, yellows, and beige are best for the camera. Black is to be avoided because it absorbs too much light. Wear knee-high socks that are darker than your pants so that you never show bare calf. Always wear a solid colored shirt and a solid colored suit or sports jacket. Only one thing can be patterned and that is your tie. Men should never get more casual than a sports jacket in lieu of a suit. Expensive-looking designer sweaters will work if the specific show and demographic of the viewer calls for it.

These rules also apply to women. Find out what color the backdrop is so your clothing does not clash. You are always safe with the neutral colors of brown, khaki, navy, and gray. Use your judgment and the opinion of at least one other person as to whether your top is see-through and whether your skirt or dress is the appropriate length. Try your wardrobe out while sitting and have someone tell you what message you look like you are trying to send. Remember, bright lights on dark cloth seem to penetrate and reveal the underwear underneath. Be careful of stripes (especially horizontal) and plaids, because a television camera makes you appear about ten pounds heavier. Avoid prints with flowers, animals, busy geometric circles or squares, and showing too much leg, or the viewers will watch the dress or body instead of listening to you.

4. Vocabulary and humor

We all know flamboyant people who not only use big words in their conversation, but just plain talk too much. In fact, we never have to worry about these people "passing gas" or "cutting cheese" because they don't shut up long enough to build up the required pressure! Although the host interviewing you may have done some research and checked out your website to become familiar with you and your message, it does not follow that the TV viewers or radio listeners have prepared themselves to tune into the program. Therefore, they don't know the unique and special jargon of your profession or the intricacies of your organization, so don't talk over their heads. Why call it "attitudinal conditioning" when you can just say "positive thinking"? Or why talk about "maldistribution of primary health care deliverers" when you can simply refer to it as a "shortage of family doctors in the country"? Military officers and NCOs are guilty, excluding non-military listeners when they talk in their infamous acronyms: "This TQM is important over in the AOR so our troops RWH."

Part of vocabulary is a sense of humor. I'm not talking about telling jokes here. I'm talking about what I call "practiced spontaneity." Long before the speech is delivered, you come up with hilarious comebacks for when something unexpected happens. If someone sneezes loudly, you immediately say, "Bless you, and that's exactly what I'm talking about. If you're going to sneeze, sneeze to the very best of your ability." Hire a humor writer to help you come up with something intimately funny about each state and each capitol city. There are only fifty of each and you should memorize your funny comments so you can interact with the audience and have something to say to every person, no matter where they are from.

This holds true with a TV or radio interview. If you have a memorized quote and answer always on the tip of your tongue, ready to use in a conversational manner in response to an interviewer's question, you come across to the viewers and listeners as one of the brightest and funniest people who ever lived. The rule with humor is that if it does not come naturally to you, don't force it—don't use it.

However, if being funny is being you, then don't shut it off when the camera or studio red light turns on. Use it and milk it in a natural way. If you're going to be plugging your book on a political talk show, memorize and practice your "spontaneity" with some quick, political one-liners. If it's a sports or educational program, make sure your repertoire includes funny comments about your interview topic and your viewing or listening audience.

5. Mind-set

When you are being interviewed on television or radio, think of yourself as an invited guest in someone's living room, politely waiting to give your opinion or factual expertise on a subject. Talk to the host or other guests in the same conversational way you would without the cameras, lights, and microphones around. If you can, imagine the camera as a person and talk directly to it whenever you make a significant point inclusive to your predetermined, specific message.

Remember, your listeners and viewers are watching you through the camera lens, and if you can glance at that lens as you would glance across a room, making eye contact with everyone present, you'll come across well. If you suddenly get a frog in your throat or an intense need to cough, don't fight it. Take care of it immediately. It happens to everybody and this demonstrates your "realness," approachability, and humanity. Remember, people connect with our imperfections, not our perfections. Simply turn away from the microphone, whether on television or radio, and cough or clear your throat. Making a "farm animal noise" is far better than choking to death and causing a real scene!

Plant yourself firmly in the chair with both feet on the ground. Sit erect so you don't create rolls around your waist. Straight-up sitting also leaves your chest cavity free and uncompressed so you can speak without running out of breath. Once you're grounded and balanced in the chair, it is good to cross your legs or ankles as it gives you a more relaxed and confident look. Never cross your arms. Whatever you bring for notes, do not try to hide them. Most of the time this builds credibility.

Chapter 11

How Do You Customize Your Speeches?

Whenever you are asked to give a speech, obviously someone issues the invitation. It is imperative, then, to be absolutely sure why they have invited you to speak. As a professional speaker, I always require a conference call with the meeting planning committee that has hired me for their convention. As I have them answer eight key questions, I can at the same time clarify in my mind what stories, research data, anecdotes, jokes, songs, poems, and personal experiences I will share in this speech that will meet their specific meeting needs. If multiple people are on the phone call, I have each of them respond to each question. In this way they take ownership of my speech and feel that they were part and proud of the decision to bring me into their organization.

The Eight Key Questions Asked on a Conference Call:

1. Do you have a specific meeting theme?

- If so, what is it?
- How did you come up with this theme?
- What does it mean to you?

2. What is the purpose of your meeting?

- Is it for motivation, training, leadership retreat, fulfillment of CEU requirements, a users group or customer event, incentive reward?

- Is this a mandatory or voluntary meeting?
- Who is paying for the conference, organization, or attendees?

3. Who are the attendees?

- What is their specific job description?
- What do they specifically do? Sales, customer service, cold calling, travel in a territory, work in a call center, manage, lead, coach, administrate, teach?
- Are they hourly labor, salaried, or commissioned?
- Are they on base-plus-commission compensation? What is the average income of the group and the highest and lowest earners in the audience (not by name but amount)?
- Who are their internal and external customers?
- Is their job more relationship or task oriented; more transactional or advisory?
- If they are in sales, how long is the sales cycle?
- Do they have a quota sales volume and minimum requirement result they must achieve quarterly or annually? What percentage of the audience has achieved these company expectations?
- What is the toughest part of their job?
- What brings them joy and satisfaction?

4. Where am I on the program?

- Am I the opening general session keynote "kick-off" speaker or the closing general session "wrap up" speaker?
- What happens right before me and right after me?
- Who else is speaking on this program?
- How many days is the conference?
- What is my time slot?
- Is it a luncheon or after-dinner speech, which needs to be lighter, funnier, and shorter than the usual sixty minutes? If the speech is after a lunch meal, the room lights should be as bright as possible to generate better energy and help keep the audience alert.
- Is my speech after a cocktail reception with alcohol or during an awards banquet?

5. Are there concurrent breakout sessions?

- If yes, what are your needs? Here's your chance to respond with:

> "Amazing! I am an expert on your desired topic and have an exciting, powerful seminar that would perfectly fit into your day. Having me stay to further develop the concepts that I delivered in my opening keynote address will keep the continuity from one session to another in place and allow me to connect more intimately with your leadership and attendees."

This is where you sell yourself as a total resource who has so much material that they should take full advantage of your expertise while you are already there. Economically it saves them other full speaker's fees and additional travel expenses and eliminates the worry of whether or not another speaker will make it there and then actually fit into the already established personality, message, and emotion of the meeting and flow of the day.

6. How did you hear about me?

- Through a Speakers Bureau? A referral by a corporate colleague who heard me? From another fellow professional speaker whom you have hired in the past?

7. Who have you had for speakers in the past?

This gives you a barometer reading of whether their commitment is to creating a sensational event using an extraordinary professional speaker or merely to a mundane meeting, recklessly willing to put the success of their gathering in the shaky hands of an ordinary amateur presenter. This question also gives you sure knowledge of what their speaker's budget is and how much they have invested in their speakers in the past. More important, it gives you the perfect opportunity to educate the meeting planning committee on your additional services and topics on which you are an expert, and recommend other professional speakers you personally know, who could help take their meeting to the ultimate level.

8. What is your desired message?

- Not if you were me, but if *you* were giving the speech. If I walked into the back of the room in this same session, what would I be hearing you say?

Each person on the conference call is asked to individually respond. I assure them I will incorporate their comments and desires into my remarks. In this way I give them ownership of my speech and make them look good to their people after I leave.

- This information also allows me to tie into key organizational buzz words and cultural clichés, which ensures that I will, in fact, accomplish the specific purposes of their meeting that they shared with me on the call.
- I also have them send me a copy of their published values, vision and mission statements, descriptions of their products and services, and anything else they think I should read and fully understand before my speech.
- I especially want to know the names of some "superstars" in the audience to whom I can pay tribute. I then memorize the key names and information and reference them in my remarks.

Five Star Service

One of the things that makes me stand out from most speakers and all presenters is the simple fact that I always attend the entire meeting the day I am speaking so that I can tie my remarks and jokes into the previous speakers and/or activities. If this surprises you, most speakers do a sound check and then show up only for their speech.

When I arrive at the venue I request to be introduced to the CEO and visit with him for fifteen minutes. I formally schedule this appointment on the conference call, and then when I meet with him on the meeting sight, the conversation is 100 percent focused on one question and one purpose. After the pleasantries I ask them the same number eight question I asked everyone on the conference call: "What is the most important message I can deliver that echoes exactly what you've been saying all year?" This serves the purpose of being able to directly quote him in my speech and gives him ownership of my message and instant credibility that I am a team player with him and am concerned about their company and cause rather than about myself. This is how you get invited back to speak again.

Chapter 12

How Do You Deliver Speeches That Listeners Will Never Forget?

After reading this far, one might think it hypocritical for me to now suggest that you formally write out and carefully structure a speech. On the contrary. After you have prepared yourself to speak, it is time to sit down, and in the case of being hired as a professional speaker, look over your conference call notes to refresh you memory of the meeting theme, purpose, attendees, and message, and write out what you wish to say. In doing so, it is of great importance to recognize that what is written to be read has a radically different character from what is written to be heard. The major difference between reading and listening is that reading allows people to proceed at their own pace and to go forward or backward at will by simply turning the pages, and listening requires them to keep moving irreversibly forward with the flow of the speech.

One of the main reasons we structure and write out a speech is to time it out. A sure sign of an amateur is to go over your allotted time slot on the program. True professional speakers always end on time. If you are given fifty-two minutes, keep your remarks to fifty-two minutes. Consequently, to fit all the parts of one's speech (Ethos, Pathos, Logos, Instruction, Persuasion, the powerful beginning, illustrative middle, and memorable conclusion) into the allotted time and to fit them together in proper proportion to one another, it is necessary to plot the organization of your speech carefully.

As we detail the following structural template, continue to remember that you spend more time preparing yourself to speak. The written speech allows you to organize your thoughts and examine your experiences in order for you to make sure you are sharing all the messages that you have learned and desire your listeners to learn from you. I have memorized my quotes and stories so that I can tell them on demand. And incidentally, the way my stories have evolved and gotten better—funnier or more emotional and deeper in meaning—is by telling them over and over again. When I say something off-the-cuff that is funny or profound, I remember it and add it to the story the next time I tell it. Without further delay, let's examine the structure of a speech that listeners will never forget.

The Six Steps of Crafting and Delivering an Unforgettable Speech:

Shhh!
Huh?
Why?
How?
Where?
When?

Shhh!

The speaker is being introduced. *Wow! Listen to this. This guy will be amazing.* Your formal introduction should be viewed as part of your speech. It should be typed, double-spaced, fourteen-point bold font, no italics, printed on your letterhead, and physically handed to the person who is going to introduce you. Most likely they have already retrieved it from your website and have included it in their master copy script for your meeting session, but this is your tactful way to make sure the organization has not taken editorial liberties and changed it.

Don't ever trust anyone else to write your introduction from your bio or a book cover. The reason you physically give a copy of your introduction to the introducer is so you can meet them and they can feel your positive energy and get excited about having you as their speaker. It also gives you the chance to tell them your introduction is part of your speech, and, therefore, they should read it verbatim. Your introduction should never be longer than sixty seconds. The longer the introduction, the more insecure the speaker! The introduction serves one purpose: to build your credibility, expose your character, and answer for each audience member the question: Why should I listen to him?

Huh?

Speaker coach Max Dixon says, "Primitive brain scans for threat. People don't buy because they understand. They buy because they are understood. Consequently, the quickest way to build authenticity and connect with the audience is to smile. When we first see you, does your behavior inspire trust and turn your attendees into listeners? To the degree this relates to likability, the most significant ingredient is the face."

The smile is the first impression and the ice breaker, followed by eye contact with many individuals, one at a time, on several different rows, which clearly sends the message that you're personable, approachable, no where else but there, and that yes, you do understand. Remember that your "home onstage" is in the faces in your audience. Finding a friendly face fast is a confidence builder, but the goal is to connect with everybody. The face will usually be the dominant thermometer of whether you are hot or cold with the crowd and the level of your rapport and connection.

In sports we know that momentum is only as good as your next play. With the momentum now created by your concise, credibility-building introduction, the most important part of your speech is the first sixty seconds. I call it "Huh?" because that's what so many of us say when we are startled out of our sleep. "Huh?" symbolizes that when we step onstage, everybody is tired, nobody wants to be in this meeting, they would rather be outside doing something fun, and why on earth would anyone make them sit there and listen to another boring lecture.

"Huh?" is the "Okay, you woke me up with the fascinating introduction, so this better be good! You've got my attention, now keep it!" For this reason, if we are given a topic to speak on such as drinking and driving, you never start your speech by saying, "I've been asked to speak on drinking and driving." This is boring, gets no one's attention, and is a typical beginning for every amateur.

Your first sixty seconds is the most important part. As the saying goes, you never get a second chance to make a first impression, so a better attention-getting technique is expected and required, such as, "One hundred thirteen teenagers were killed this weekend." If your assigned topic is wearing seat belts, you don't begin by saying, "I've been assigned to talk to you about the importance of wearing your seat belt." A better "Huh?"

attention getter is a shocker like, "A friend of mine, who is the proud father of nine children, killed his two youngest daughters last Wednesday." I guarantee in both of these examples every audience member immediately becomes a listener!

Why?

Why did you bring this up? How does it relate to me? If you visualize each audience member as being stranded on a broken barge floating amid the ocean waves with no working rudder or steering mechanism, it becomes obvious that you must throw them a line to bring them back into shore. This "Why?" step is the connection that bridges the gap between you onstage and your listeners in the audience. This is the next sixty seconds of your speech—the second most important part of your first impression—the next play you must definitely make in order to keep the momentum alive that was created in your introduction and carried on in the previous "Huh?" step.

The next "Why?" step is based on not only the bridge from your mind and heart to your audience members' minds and hearts, but it is also at the very core of leading, managing, coaching, teaching, parenting, inspiring, motivating, and persuading anyone for any occasion and for every reason. This is the first place you actually prove you are a professional speaker instead of just a professional presenter. "Why?" is when you first customize your message to the meeting theme, purpose, and audience attendees. This is when you start making this time you are spending with your listeners relevant to their circumstances, jobs, industry, and lives. This most enlightening quote that is at the heart of sales, customer service, and especially public speaking is one I already quoted for a different reason in a previous chapter: "The only place from which a person can grow is where he or she is. We must go where they are physically and emotionally." Only there can we gently persuade and instruct them to grow. Only there can we invite them to trust our character, listen, and learn from us.

Let us put both the "Huh?" attention getter and "Why?" connection-bridging lines together for illustration: "One hundred thirteen teenagers were killed this weekend. Not one was drinking alcohol, but all died in drinking and driving accidents. Two teenagers from a town close by were driving home late when most bars are closing down, like Torre's just down the street, and a drunk guy ran a stop sign, hit them broadside going seventy miles an hour, and killed this seventeen-year-old kid and his high school sweetheart. Do any of you have teenagers? These two young friends were buried close to each other in the same cemetery."

Or, "A friend of mine, who is the proud father of nine children, killed his two youngest daughters last Wednesday. They were only eight and ten years old, and, as their father, he was responsible to make sure they were wearing their seat belts. On Wednesday my friend was a lousy dad, and because his little girls were not wearing their seat belts, when a car ran a stop sign and hit their car, his precious little angels were thrown out of the car and killed instantly. He got out of the hospital just in time to attend their funerals."

Because it is the speaker's responsibility to go out of their way to connect with each audience member and turn them into listeners, let me illustrate this "the only place we can connect with others is where they are" principle with a story. I was recently visiting with Mr. Croft, my former high school teacher. We were discussing mutual respect and support in the context of positive discipline. I was looking for a firsthand experience from the world of education that would apply to parenting, coaching, and the corporate world of management, sales, and customer service.

The conversation centered on how to motivate, inspire, and empower others—not only to increase performance and productivity but to follow the rules and show respect. Mr. Croft asked for my definitions. With regard to mutual respect and support, I said, "The only place from which a person can grow is where he or she is." As for positive discipline, I said, "You cannot increase a person's performance by making him or her feel worse; humiliation immobilizes behavior."

Mr. Croft's eyes lit up with excitement as he shared the following experience to illustrate this point.

"I had a student who disrupted everything," he said.

"Did you send him to the office?" I asked.

With an offended look on his face, he said, "I've taught school for over twenty-five years and I've never sent a student to the principal." Mr. Croft laughed. "Most of my colleagues think the principal has all the Band-Aids. No way. Teachers are responsible for their classrooms and the development and education of each kid. You don't just throw them out when they do something wrong. We have to invite them to grow. We must catch them doing something right."

"Mr. Croft," I interrupted, "I've been to schools where a long line of students trails out the principal's office, down the hall, out the door and past the 9A bus stop. They're suntanned! And they just stand there with that look of 'yep, I screwed a goldfish into the pencil sharpener four months ago and I'm still waiting to see the principal.' If this is education, we're fooling ourselves! So what did you do with your student?" I asked.

"Interesting you should ask," he replied. "I didn't give up on him. My research uncovered that this James character played in a rock-and-roll band and that he was playing that Friday night in a smoke-filled, honky-tonk, redneck biker bar out in the bushes somewhere. I talked five teachers into going with me in case I needed back-up."

"Then what happened?" I asked.

"Now picture this," Mr. Croft continued. "Six of us in argyle sweaters with matching socks stood at the back of the dance floor surrounded by teenagers who looked like they'd been mugged with a staple gun. The lead singer had a carburetor stuck in his nose. When James spotted us he leaned into the microphone and asked, 'What are you proctologist-looking teachers doing here?' We told him we heard his band was awesome and wanted to check them out. My colleagues and I only stayed fifteen minutes. That's all the noise we could take."

That was Friday night. On Monday morning was James a discipline problem in Mr. Croft's class? No way. Was he a problem in Mr. Croft's class for the rest of the school year? No way! Was James a discipline problem in other teachers' classrooms for the rest of the school year? Yes! Was it because they couldn't teach? No. It was simply because they didn't care! Positive discipline means caring about a person physically and emotionally—and catching that person doing something right!

How?

Give me the proof! Tell me the stories. Share the emotional, funny, and thought-provoking experiences and research data that give me the hope that I can actually go from where I am to where I want to be. Help me see through illustrations that what one person or organization has done really is possible; that if I think and behave and believe and conceive the same as a specific champion did, I too can become a champion.

Stories and parables are the parts of the speech that grab them and keep the attendees listening. They constitute the entertaining, emotional portion that they remember and can't wait to share with family, coworkers, and friends who did not hear you speak. This fourth "How?" step is best delivered through a process of "make a statement, make a point, and then use 'for instance' to sharpen your point." Then do it again. Make another point and illustrate it.

One of the most popular and easiest resources to illustrate "How?" is history. And because most presenters focus on the over-used examples from history, such as Abraham Lincoln's failing his way to success and Edison discovering 999 ways that a light bulb won't work, why not dig up some new, unique "for instances"? Especially when you are given topics like racism. Instead of doing the predictable or focusing on the victims and negative struggles for equality, why not take the surprising, positive high road and use fascinating examples from history? Elijah McCoy was a gifted engineer who happened to be the son of slaves. During his lifetime he was awarded forty-five patents. In 1872, he invented a device to make steam engines run more smoothly. For a while the market resisted McCoy's invention—no doubt feeling it couldn't work if it was designed by a black man. But competitors couldn't match his results, so buyers began asking, "Is this the real McCoy?"

Inventions from Blacks

Paper—Africans
Alphabet—Africans
Coin changer—James A. Bauer
Rotary engine—Andrew J. Beard
Stainless-steel pads—Alfred Benjamin
Home security system—Marie Brown
Ironing board—Sarah Boone
Street sweepers—C. B. Brooks
Horseshoe—Oscar E. Brown
Lawn mower—John A. Burr
Typewriter—Burridge & Marshman
Peanut butter—George W. Carver
Soap and lotion—George W. Carver
Pressure cooker—Maurice W. Lee
Window cleaner—A. L. Lewis
Pencil sharpener—John L. Love
Fire extinguisher—Tom J. Marshal
Player piano—Joseph Dickinson
Toilet (commode)—T. Elkins

Gas mask—Garrett Morgan
Guitar—Robert Flemming Jr.
Air conditioner—Frederick M. Jones
Internal combustion engine—Frederick M. Jones
Refrigerator—J. Standard
Mop—T. W. Stewart
Elevator—Alexander Miles
Folding chair—Purdy & Sadgwar
Baby buggy—W. H. Richardson
Lawn sprinkler—J. W. Smith

Women don't get enough credit for the part they played in the American Revolution. We've all heard of Betsy Ross and how she made the first American flag, but women have been in the thick of things since the beginning. One brave young woman was only sixteen when she took a midnight ride as dangerous and exciting—but far less publicized—as Paul Revere's. On the night of April 25, 1777, two thousand British soldiers began destroying rebel storehouses. They found rum among the supplies, got drunk and started burning the town. A wounded messenger rode to a farm twenty miles from the town. The man who lived on the farm was the captain of the local militia. If he left to warn the surrounding cities, he would not be able to lead his four hundred volunteers into battle. His daughter, Sybil, offered to go in his place. Mounted sidesaddle, she rode forty miles—twice as far as Paul Revere—through a perilous region filled with hostile Indians. As she traveled, she shouted warnings and banged on doors with a stout branch to alert the townspeople along the way. It took Sybil all night to make her ride.

Women have always been brave, heroic, and patriotic. Sadly, we don't hear as much about their acts as we should. It's time we realized that heroes aren't just men. The choreography of emotion can never be perceived as a cavalier way to manipulate another's thoughts and feeling. If this is the purpose of your story, poem, or comments, I guarantee your audience members will see right through it, feel violated, and turn you off for the rest of your speech.

However, if you take them to a certain high level through laughter, you are subconsciously given the right to take them to an equally low level in tears, as long as you don't keep them hurting. In other words, if your words make someone hurt, it's okay as long as you also help them heal.

Let us never back down from the reality that the things we hate to hear the most are usually the things we need to hear the most.

Failure is an event, not a person. There is a huge difference between the person and the performance. You invite your listeners to feel and internally excavate their personal lives through your stage-conducted self-audit. To assure you that it's okay and actually very responsible of you as a speaker to go deeper and perhaps even open up some old wounds in your listeners' past and present lives, let me share this medical understanding on healing.

Speaker as Healer

When we understand medicine and music from the inside-out perspective, it is easy to fully comprehend the process of healing. We all know that doctors can't and don't heal anyone. Through the administration of medication and the performance of surgery, they help us heal ourselves. Physicians are not gods or miracle workers; they are catalysts and caregivers. Having said this, let's clarify the process of healing. There are two kinds of healing—healing by "First Intention" and by "Second Intention."

Healing by the First Intention is outside healing where there is a scratch or superficial, shallow wound with a straight edge opening that quickly coagulates, stops bleeding, and heals with a few stitches to close the cut or with just a Band-Aid to keep it clean. Name calling, gossip, and rumors are "scuffed knees" and "paper cuts" that can and will always heal from the outside-in.

Healing by Second Intention is inside-out healing, where the wound is deep, the edges jagged, and the gouge uncertain. In this case if you only stop the surface bleeding, stitch the surface layer of skin, and bandage it to heal from the outside-in, underneath it all and unbeknownst to you, the wound is festering, infection is setting in, and gangrene could result in the amputation of that limb. When we suffer and experience a deep gouge wound—a stabbing, the bursting of our appendix, a broken heart, the loss of a loved one, a devastating divorce, being let go from a job—the only way we can heal is if we keep the wound open long enough with the proper treatment—kindness and care—until it can slowly, in its own time, heal from the inside-out, one layer, one step at a time.

A professional speaker does this by sharing a heart-warming story that re-opens a deep wound in an audience member. They keep the deep wound open just long enough to let some healing occur, but then, because they are in a public setting, the professional speaker closes the wound by providing comic relief immediately afterward.

This "How?" middle section of the speech that offers the "for instances" is the glue that binds the introduction, which states you're an expert in this or a master storyteller or are personally experienced, to the first sixty seconds of your attention-getting "Huh?" and to the follow-up minute that answers, "Why bring that up?" Something as redundant as speaking on drinking and driving, which has been crammed down young people's throats for decades, can actually be presented in a powerful, emotionally stirring, less preachy, more sharing way when we take full advantage of this "How" step and utilize the long-lasting third party approach found in a story or a poem:

Steve was careful about his drinking because his wife, Melba, worried. She said liquor made him too confident and not cautious. *Women never really understand their men*, he thought. Instead, they always worry about things that never happen. Steve snapped up the shot glass, tilted his head, and nodded to the bartender as he left.

Outside he thought about how happy he was. Steve owned a house and Melba was pregnant again. He hoped it would be a girl since they already had an eighteen-month-old son. Steve was hurrying to pick up Melba at the doctor's office. Although the car skidded slightly on the icy roads, he wanted to hurry since he'd stopped at the bar. He sped up a notch, then suddenly realized he couldn't make the turn at the bottom of the hill. The car was headed for the guard rail that was set around the edge of the lake. To compensate, Steve propped his door open with his briefcase so he could get out when the car hit. He planned to jump out and swim to the bank.

People saw the car coming and watched as it splashed into the water. As he planned, Steve got out safely and swam for shore. People cheered when he arrived safely. He thought, *See, I can handle my liquor.* As he stood there smiling, waving to the crowd, and watching his car submerge, Steve's heart sank. His little boy, Jared, was still strapped in his car seat in the back of the car.

It's Nobody's Business What I Drink

It's nobody's business what I drink!
I care not what the neighbors think.

Or how many laws they choose to pass!
I'll tell the world, "I'll have my glass!"

Here's one man's freedom that cannot be curbed;
My right to drink is undisturbed.
So he drank in spite of law or man,
Then got into his old tin can:

Stepped on the gas and let it go,
Down the highway to and fro.
He took the curves at 50 miles
With bleary eyes and drunken smiles.

Not long till a car he tried to pass;
There was a crash, a scream, and breaking glass.
The other car was upside down,
About two miles from the nearest town.

The man was clear but his wife was caught,
And she needed the help of that drunken sot,
Who sat in a maudlin, drunken daze,
And heard the scream and saw the blaze,

The car was burned and the mother died,
While a husband wept and baby cried,
And a drunk sat by—and still some think
It's nobody's business what they drink!

Don't Be Afraid to Shock

Shock factor is an extremely effective way to illustrate a mundane topic like responsibility and thinking before you act. A man came out of his home to admire his new truck. To his puzzlement, his three-year-old son was happily hammering dents into the shiny paint. The man ran to his son, knocked him away, and hammered the little boy's hands into a pulp as punishment.

When the father calmed down, he rushed his son to the hospital. Although the doctor tried desperately to save the crushed bones, he finally had to amputate the fingers from both of the boy's hands. When the child woke up from surgery and saw his bandaged stubs, he innocently said, "Daddy, I'm sorry about your truck." Then he asked, "But when are my fingers going to grow back?"

The father went home and committed suicide. Think about this story the next time you see someone spill milk at the dinner table or hear a baby crying. Think first before you lose your patience with someone you love. Trucks can be repaired. Broken bones and hurt feelings often can't.

Too often we fail to recognize the difference between the person and the performance. People make mistakes. We are allowed to make mistakes. But the actions we take while in a rage will haunt us forever. Pause and ponder. Think before you act. Be patient. Understand and love.

An Alaskan trapper lost his wife and was left to care for his two-year-old daughter. At times he had to leave the little girl with his faithful dog so he could work in the woods. While away one afternoon a terrible blizzard came up. The trapper was forced to take refuge in a hollow tree. At daybreak he rushed to his cabin and found the door was open. His dog was covered with blood. There was no little girl anywhere. The father was terrified that something awful had happened. Fearful that his dog had killed and eaten his child, the trapper reached for his ax.

In one swift move he smashed the skull of his loyal and trusted canine companion. Like a maniac he tore through the cabin searching for his missing girl. Suddenly a faint cry came from under the bed. There was his daughter, safe and sound. Looking further he found the bloody remains of a wolf in the corner. Then he knew—the dog had saved the child from the fangs of the wolf. If he had only stopped to assess the situation rationally, the trapper could have held both his child and his dog in his arms. Weigh all factors before you make a move.

Those who act hastily regret their actions later. It happens all the time. Judgments made irrationally are clouded by a lack of information. The whole picture is hazy. So get the facts before you act.

The flip side of these heart-wrenching stories is an equally instructive use of a song:

Special Man

A little boy wants to be like his dad
So he watches us night and day.
He mimics our moves and weighs our words.
He steps in our steps all the way.

He's sculpting a life we're the model for.
He'll follow us happy or sad,
And his future depends on example set
'Cause the little boy wants to be just like his dad.

A special man talks by example,
Takes the time to play and hug his lad.
A special man walks by example,
The very best friend a growing boy ever had.
Any male can be a father—
But it takes a special man to be a dad.

He needs a hero to emulate.
He breathes 'I believe in you.'
Would we have him see everything we see
And have him do what we do?

When we see the reverence that sparkles and shines
In the worshipping eyes of our lad,
Will we be at peace if his dreams come true
And he grows up to be just like his dad?

Yes, a special man talks by example,
Takes the time to play and hug his lad.
A special man walks by example,
The very best friend a growing boy ever had.
Any male can be a father—
But it takes a special man to be a dad.

This "How?" step moves us to change our thinking and kicks us in the butt, encouraging us to think before we act and look inside for happiness. Why is the grass always greener somewhere else? Some people spend their whole lives looking for happiness when it's right under their noses. Teenagers run away looking for a better life, but they rarely find it. Divorce is rampant. The truth is happiness is where you are—you make your own.

In the mid eighteen hundreds, a man sold his ranch in northern California to look for gold nuggets. The new owner put a mill on a stream that ran through the property. One day the new owner's little girl brought home some sand from the stream in a jar and sifted through it. In the sand were the first shiny nuggets of gold to be found in California. If the man had stayed put, he could have had all the gold he ever needed. Since that day, thirty-eight million dollars in gold has been taken out of those few acres he sold.

It's better to try to make the most of what you have before trying to find happiness elsewhere. Maybe what can really make you happy is just hidden from your sight, temporarily out of view for a while. So look hard. Dig in where you are before you sell. Study the problems that might be pushing you away from your loved ones before you leave something very important behind.

Use Illustrations Everybody Can Relate To

"How?" brings the magic into the moment. Therefore, amid all of these shocking stories, it is critical to remind you not only of the importance of humor and that we all love to laugh a heck of a lot more than we want to cry but also that a speech structured, crafted, and written so listeners like it and will never forget it must have a funny story for every sad one.

"He who laughs, lasts." It's a medical fact that if you keep your sense of humor, you'll probably live longer. Even large corporations realize the truth in it. Monsanto, the chemical giant, hired a humor consultant to work with research scientists. Productivity increased 50 percent. Digital Equipment designed a Grouch Patrol to make funny faces at grumpy workers. Productivity went up; absenteeism went down. Bertrand Russell said, "One of the symptoms of an approaching nervous breakdown is the belief that one's work is terribly important." So lighten up!

Two of my favorite humorous observations are:

Observation #1

I'm losing hair on top of my head and growing it in my nose and ears. My only hope is that the hair in my right ear will grow long enough so I can comb it up over my head and fake everybody out.

Observation #2

You take a big heavy ball, cram two fingers and a thumb in it, take four Fred Flintstone twinkle-toes steps, roll the ball, sit down, eat a hot dog, have something to drink, and for this you need special shoes? And because they think we're going to steal the shoes, they make us leave a cash deposit. Now I don't know about you, but I don't own a green and purple shirt that's going to match those goofy shoes, and I definitely don't want to be seen walking around town with an 11½ on the back of my foot!

Where?

As in, "Where do I go from here? Where is this system of success that others have used, which, if I also use, will work for me?" The system is the Twelve-Step Program made famous by Alcoholics Anonymous. In this "Where?" step, you simply use your credibility to convince your listeners that neither an individual nor an organization can change with just a one-hour keynote speech, that training is not an expense, but rather an investment in the present and future of the organization.

"Where?" is the place in the speech when you give out your website and explain that if they are serious about taking themselves to the next level, they will join you at your weekend seminar or retreat, buy your book, and bring you back for a full day of leadership, team building, sales, or customer service training. Because you firmly believe in what you are passionately persuading your listeners to do, you shamelessly offer everyone your products and follow-up services. You absolutely know you can change people's minds and show them how to become everything they were born to be!

As you now realize, audience members are craving a sustainable, emotional, personal experience—not just a speech. They don't want a presenter to deliver a talking-head monologue. They want to be part of an inspirational conversation where they feel you are genuinely there to help them become better, and because of this connection they want to maintain contact with you in every way available. This is why we should unashamedly offer our recorded and written resources to them.

Most meeting planners realize that when a speaker has had one or more books published, this is proof that he has researched and become an expert on that topic. The book builds the credibility of the speaker. Most meeting planners also realize that a one-hour keynote speech or ninety-minute seminar cannot change anybody or anything for a sustained period of time. I find it ironic, then, that some meeting planners are reluctant to allow the speaker to sell his book or materials after the presentation.

The speech or seminar is only one piece of the total solution. The speech is the introduction to the meeting theme and a catalyst for change, but because the teacher appears *only* when the student is ready, we can't expect everybody to get it, feel it, and take action on the speech or seminar until they are ready within their own emotional, "need to change" time frame.

For these reasons, speakers who have written books or course curriculums should never feel intimidated by the false assumption that audience members will be offended if you sell your products from the platform. Your book is another critical piece of the total solution that you are bringing to the relationship. Your book is the "take away," the necessary component that truly becomes the teacher when the student is ready, sometimes hours, days, or weeks after the speech has been delivered.

Two Proven Product-Selling Suggestions

1. Pre-sell. When the meeting planner books you on the program, suggest they purchase your book for each attendee. The following dialogue has successfully worked for my office: "I am thrilled to see that you have secured Dan for your June 16 meeting and look forward to working with you on this event. I'd like to send you a proposal with a copy of each of Dan's books for you to review and decide if you're interested in gifting one or more to your audience members. I'm sure anyone attending Dan's session would be delighted with such a great take-away gift. Each time a story or principle is read or shared, Dan's messages of empowerment, productivity, and positive attitude will be brought home again and again—a pretty powerful motivational tool that will keep Dan's philosophy on passionate living current long after his keynote speech has ended." If the meeting planners simply do not want to or don't have the budget to pre-buy, then offer to host a book signing after your presentation, at no cost to the client, where the audience members can choose to buy your products after your presentation.

2. To sell from the platform with confidence, you must honestly believe you are providing a vital resource and will be giving the audience an unfinished program unless they take home your book (as if they are leaving an award-winning three-act play at the end of the second act!). We speakers are there to make a difference. It's true that most attendees didn't come expecting to buy. They assumed they would just sit there and—*abracadabra!*—magically change. But if the speaker doesn't give them

everything he knows to help them take it to the next level, the speaker is doing a disservice. Our products are there to reinforce and expand on what we can cover in the brief time we spend on the platform.

So the attendees don't feel "sold to" (which translates into them being offended and not responding to back-of-the-room sales), we need only couch our resource pitch as the way to have us there with them at work and home to support them as they try to change. It's about providing practical and applicable value beyond your hour together and the content of your speech.

Meeting Planner Objection

What if the meeting planner does not pre-purchase, order your book, or allow you to host a signing or mention your products from the platform? What works for me is to have a copy of my book at the podium and, during the course of my speech, ask at least two provocative questions, and then pause while I quickly look up the answers in my book. Reading a powerful quote, sharing specific statistics, or relating a poem or song lyric that they can't get any other place sparks the attendees' curiosity to want to get their hands on the source of this unique information. It's also valuable to include something like, "I don't have time to cover all twelve concepts that are included in my book, so let me just share four." Then read the four steps straight from the book and casually close it and discuss. Guaranteed, this technique is the best option when pitching from the stage is not allowed.

Best Sales and Marketing Close

Immediately before you go into the powerful conclusion to your speech, the following offer should be made: "Before I close, let me express my thanks to each of you for being here and extend a sincere plea that if there is anything else I can do to help you make the changes you seek in your life, meet me in the back of the room when this session is over and I'll share some additional ways I can be of service." If you don't have books or handouts, this is where you provide order forms and contact information, reminding them that the package they can get through your office is the total program solution to what they experienced with you that day. With this "I must maintain contact" seed now planted in their minds and hearts, go into your planned practiced speech conclusion remembering what I've cited before, "Reason leads to conclusions, but it is emotion that leads to action!"

Last, "Where?" is the performance, entertainment component of your speech that causes your audience members to sit on the edge of their seats because they don't want to miss any part of your show. They constantly wonder, "Where will he take me next?"

Taking an audience on an exciting, emotional, up-and-down roller coaster ride is an art and requires special skills. These are the "mechanical moves" and "tangible tools" that polish the performance. They constitute the differentiating factors between a professional speaker and a Hall of Fame Consummate Speaker. In the Kentucky Derby, all horses are thoroughbreds. However, amidst all the champions entered in the race, only one wins this run for the roses and is crowned Derby winner. So likewise, there are a lot of professional speakers, but to be one of the best of the best and right for every audience, industry, and occasion, you need to perfect the following eight platform skills.

Eight Platform Skills

1. Get eye contact with your audience members. Listeners like to feel they are influencing what you say. Audience reaction is an essential ingredient in this whole business of speaking. What you see on their faces or in their eyes tells you instantly whether you are getting across. Such feedback is indispensable to being a professional speaker.

2. Make sure your stage moves have purpose. Avoid body-swaying, weight-shifting, finger fidgeting, hair and clothing adjusting, and moving around too quickly and too much. When making your most significant points, always begin in the back half of center stage and move forward toward the audience. This psychologically hits home to your listeners that this point is critical.

3. Gesture. Use your hands to describe space and distance. If you are talking about something far away, in the future or visionary, extend your arm fully and point outward and upward if necessary. Use your hands to show the height and size of a person or thing. Use several fingers to count and keep the audience on track. Use an arm pump to accentuate and both arms up to signal touchdown, victory, "oh yeah." Shrug your shoulders with your palms up to punctuate Who knows? Who cares? and What's up? Use your body to illustrate and bring your characters to life. Use your imagination and let your inhibitions run wild in doing that which is necessary with your body to help your mouth paint the word pictures.

4. Talk. Don't lecture, exhort, expound, or try to baffle the audience with your B.S. using multi-syllable vocabulary words. Talk with the same conversational inflections that you use in your home. Change the pitch of your voice. Give your listeners high pitches and low pitches full of unpredictable valleys and peaks. Change the volume of your voice. In every sentence you deliver there's at least one word that deserves selective emphasis. Yell, whisper, call out, quietly confide, reverently honor, and humbly plead—modulate your voice.

5. Enunciate clearly. Focus your vocal pitch and volume on three representative people in each audience: the bored guy on the last row, the old man with the hearing aid in the middle of the room, and the foreign guest on the front row who doesn't understand English very well. Change the speed of your delivery. Talk clearly, loudly, and slowly enough that all three types of people just mentioned do not have to strain to hear you, understand you, be instructed, persuaded, and inspired.

6. Perfect the punctuating pause. If you tell a story where the person dies at the end, pause and let him die. Let the audience feel the raw emotion before you move on. The same holds true with a joke. After you deliver the punch line, pause and let the audience laugh and enjoy themselves. Never start in too soon with more words. Let the listener wallow in the silence for an uncomfortable moment. Let the listener laugh until the laughter dies down. Only then should you proceed with your speech. No one likes to be cut off from enjoying the emotion of the moment. Stepping on the laughs or tears has the same emotional effect on us as having someone interrupt us just as we begin to sneeze a wonderful mighty sneeze!

7. Be animated. Don't be afraid to pull faces, momentarily wear a prop, or go out in the audience to interact. The one eyebrow lift, the deer-in-the-headlights stare, the jaw drop "Oh my gosh," the blank stupid stare "I don't get it," and so forth. Don't be afraid to shock the audience by suddenly running across the stage or jumping up and down. For the dramatic effect, I personally kneel down on one knee at a key moment in every speech to get more intimate, up close, and personal with the listeners about a significant point I am making.

8. Close with impeccability. Just as their first impressions of you from your introduction must be congruent with your public persona that walks out onstage, so likewise must their last impressions be congruent with the speech your listeners just heard. As Max Dixon says, "Give your best expression, your best word choice to your close and it will anchor a deep satisfaction between you and your audience." Give them an emotional amen, a quotable quote you personally wrote, and a memory of their experience with you that will echo in their minds, stir their souls, and be worthy of sharing long after the meeting adjourns.

Emotional Close

Usually the one idea and feeling that your audience members remember most is their last impression. Consequently, I usually close my speeches in a mellow, inspirational way that allows the listeners to re-enter the outside world reality with a smooth transition. As an audience member myself, I personally enjoy an emotional, heartfelt, deeply moving story that illustrates once and for all the bottom line message of the speech. My friend and colleague Mark Victor Hansen has often used a powerful story that he and I affectionately refer to as "Bopsy."

Bopsy was a young boy living in Phoenix, Arizona, dying of terminal leukemia. At the present time there is absolutely no cure. One day his mother had the presence of mind to ask him, "Bopsy, if you had one wish, what would it be?" Without even thinking about it, Bopsy replied, "Mommy, if I had one wish and I knew it would come true, I'd want to be a fireman."

The next morning, Bopsy's mother phoned the local fire department and talked to the fire chief. She explained her son's health condition and his wish. The fire chief had a heart as big as a house and answered, "I'd love to make Bopsy's dream come true. You tell him that we'll be by to pick him up at 8:00 a.m. We'll make him honorary fire chief for the whole day." The fire chief continued, "If you'll give me Bopsy's measurements, I'll have a helmet made for him just like the big guys wear. We'll have a yellow slicker jacket and rubber galoshes for him too."

Sure enough, at 8:00 a.m the fire engine pulled up in front of Bopsy's house. They helped him get all decked out in his very own fireman's uniform, and that day he got to go on two fire calls. It inspired him to the depth of his being, so that he lived three months longer than any doctor thought he could possibly live.

On the last night of Bopsy's short life, the head nurse in the hospital was monitoring his vital signs and noticed they were starting to weaken. Bopsy's parents's eyes filled with tears as they knew his short life was coming to an end. Scrambling to help in any way she could, the nurse remembered the relationship Bopsy had developed with the local fire department. Immediately she phoned the fire chief and told him, "Bopsy is not doing too good and I thought you would like to know. Maybe there is something you could do for him."

The fire chief shouted, "You tell that little guy to hang on. We will be there in five minutes. But, nurse, there are a couple of things we need you to do for us. Will you please announce over the PA system of the hospital that everyone is going to hear the sirens screaming and see the lights flashing, and that we are coming to see our boy Bopsy for the last time. And would you please open up the third-story window to Bopsy's hospital room, because this time we're coming by hook and ladder!"

Moments later the sirens were screaming, the lights were flashing, and the fire engines pulled up to the hospital. A huge ladder went up the side of the building. Ten firemen and two firewomen scampered up the ladder and climbed through the third-story window into Bopsy's hospital room. They kissed him and cuddled him. With tears streaming down everyone's cheeks, the big, burly fire chief leaned over Bopsy's hospital bed and took hold of his frail little hand. With a big smile on his precious, innocent face, Bopsy looked up at the fire chief and with his last breath asked, "Chief, am I now really a fireman?"

The fire chief answered, "Bopsy, you are." And the little guy died.

An awesome emotional close, eh? But only if you link it back into the chain of points and stories you've shared. For example, my conclusive commentary would be: Can you now see and feel the power of a dream? I know this story of Bopsy resonates with everyone, young and old, because each of us has a dream stuck inside still unfulfilled. So, I guess the concluding question is, "What are you going to do about your dream?" It's like they say in the movie *South Pacific*, "If you don't have a dream, how ya gonna have a dream come true?"

President Ronald Reagan put it better than anyone I've ever heard. Right after he had been shot in an assassination attempt, and realizing how precious life is, and, like Bopsy, that no one knows when our last day will be, he said, "America was founded on a dream, and now it's your turn to keep that dream moving. We've always reached for a new spirit and aimed at a higher goal. We've always been courageous, determined, unafraid, and bold. Who among us ever wants to say we no longer have those qualities?

We look to you to meet the great challenge, to reach beyond the commonplace and not fall short for lack of creativity and courage. And to do this? All you need to begin with is a dream to do better than ever before. All you need is to have faith and that dream will come true. All you need to do is act, and the time for action is now! Go for it and good night!"

"When?"

"When?" is the conclusion that ties a bow around your speech. The "When?" step is "When are you going to do something with what I've just talked about?" It's the call to action. We don't learn to know; we learn to do. It doesn't do us any good to know how to read if we never pick up a book and read it. It doesn't do us any good to listen to a speaker if we never accept their challenge to change. It doesn't do a speaker any good to speak for sixty minutes with a great opening and great illustrations if they leave their listeners hanging in the air. "That's it? He's done? The speech is over? So what? He's 'left the building' and I have no new direction or clearer path to walk when I leave this meeting."

"When?" is the challenge. It's not the proverbial "meaningful poem." It's a direct invitation for each listener to immediately do something with what they have felt and heard, learned and assimilated into their souls. In the "How?" step we encouraged the making of a point and the sharpening of that point with illustrations, historical stories, and statistics.

Now we come to the conclusion of the speech. The very end of your speech, like the end of the proverbial pencil, should have a point. The conclusion must be more than a review of your "for instances." It must be more than a graceful exit offstage. And most definitely it should never be a cutesy gimmick to get people to give you a standing ovation.

Conclude by asking your listeners for some specific action that is within their current capacity and personal power to perform: Vote! Forgive! Join! Participate! Execute! Buy! Improve! Love! Serve! Lead! Follow! Become more of who you already are—not because it is expected by others, but because it is demanded of yourself! We must never forget that we cannot coach results, we can only coach behavior. We can't say, "Go out and win; go sell more." We can only say, "If you perfectly practice and polish your skill set, and take this new information and this emotional and inspirational attitude adjustment to heart, you will greatly increase your chances of winning and selling more!"

Why be an average, professional presenter when you can be a consummate polished professional speaker? Go ahead. Wait no longer. Take advantage of the *Privilege of the Platform*. Study, practice, and perfect the art and science of public speaking. You now know how to be a powerful communicator, how to write and organize customized speeches, how to give an amazing media interview, and how and why you can become a professional speaker who makes a great living and a lasting difference.

Welcome aboard this communication ship and hopefully you will stay aboard by officially joining the National Speakers Association headquartered in Phoenix, Arizona (www.nsaspeaker.org). Once you join NSA, I hope you will actively participate in your local NSA chapter that holds monthly meetings in your area, presenting fabulous guest speakers and awesome workshops on how to become the best speaker you can possibly be. For the local NSA chapter near you, call 480-968-2552.

It's time for all of us to become better communicators and change the world one meeting, one person, one story at a time!

The End

(Which is the beginning.)

Dan Clark is the CEO of a multi-million-dollar corporation, an internationally recognized speaker, a songwriter/recording artist, and a *New York Times* best selling author. Dan serves on the International Board of Governors of Operation Smile and on the National Advisory Board for OK Kids Charities.

In the last twenty-five years, Dan has spoken to more than 4,000 audiences and to more than 3.5 million people in all fifty states and in thirty-five countries. "Achievers North America" and "Achievers Europe" named Dan one of the Top Ten Speakers in the World. In 2005 Dan was inducted into the National Speakers Association Hall of Fame.

Dan is the primary contributing author to the *Chicken Soup for the Soul* series and author of twenty of his own best selling books, including the highly acclaimed *Forgotten Fundamentals—The Answers Are in the Box*. Dan's story "Puppies for Sale" was made into a film starring the late Jack Lemmon at Paramount Studios. As a master storyteller, Dan has been published in more than 30 million books in 30 languages worldwide!

Check out Dan Clark's website at www.danclarkspeak.com